CURIOSITIES
OF THE
California Desert

CURIOSITIES

OF THE

California Desert

HISTORIC, OFFBEAT & FORGOTTEN ATTRACTIONS

CLAUDIA & ALAN HELLER

THE
History
PRESS

Published by The History Press
Charleston, SC 29403
www.historypress.net

Unless otherwise noted, photographs are by Alan Heller.

First published 2015

Manufactured in the United States

ISBN 978.1.46711.837.8

Library of Congress Control Number: 2015946394

For our grandchildren:
Sierra Francis
Hailey Noel
Joseph Alan Cole
Kirra Michelle
Taj Beau

Contents

Foreword, by Emmett Harder   11

Acknowledgements   13

Introduction   15

PART 1: CURIOSITIES AND ODDITIES

Salvation Mountain and Slab City   19

Giant Rock and Integratron   22

The Giant Intaglios of Blythe   26

Burro Schmidt's Tunnel: Obsession or Folly?   28

The Giant Thermometer of Baker   30

The Curious Desert View Tower   32

Cabot Yerxa and His Pueblo   33

The Mystic Maze   35

Devils Hole and the Plight of the Desert Pupfish   37

Anza-Borrego's Many Curiosities   44

Peg Leg Smith   48

Cowboy Man of Mecca   51

The Mojave Cross   53

Pinnacles of Trona   55

Teakettle Junction and the Racetrack   57

Singing Eureka Dunes   58

CONTENTS

PART II: VISITING HISTORY

Willie Boy's Grave   61
Wyatt Earp's Home, Mine   64
Where the Hell Is Cerro Gordo?   67
Randsburg   71
Zzyzx   74
Goffs: An Oddity of Oddities   78
Historic Keys Ranch   81
Kelso Station and Dunes   83
Charm of Nipton   85
Mitchell Caverns   86
Ballarat   88
Pioneertown   90
Antelope Valley Indian Museum   92
China Ranch and Date Farm   93
Darwin   94
Trona's Dirt   96

PART III: REMNANTS OF ROUTE 66

Elmer's Bottle Tree Ranch   99
Polly Gas Sign   100
Auto Club Fountain   101
The Stone Hotel   102
Fouts' Garage   103
California Agricultural Station   103

PART IV: HISTORIC CEMETERIES

Bagdad   105
Shoshone   107
Amboy   108

PART V: HISTORIC OASES

Oasis of Mara   109
Thousand Palm Oasis   110
Palm Canyon Oasis   111

PART VI: DESERT ART

Coso Petroglyphs   113
Granite Mountain Pictographs   115

CONTENTS

Cabazon Dinosaurs 116
Twentynine Palms Murals 117
Barstow Murals 118
Danby Mural 119

PART VII: TRANSIENT ROADSIDE ANOMALIES
Shoe, Bra and Panty Trees 121
Rock Art 123
Painted Rocks 123

PART VIII: VANISHED DESERT ODDITIES
Loneliest Telephone Booth 125
The Camel Brigade 127
Farewell, Marilyn 128

Index 131
About the Authors 135

Foreword

I am an adventurer, writer and historian, and I love the California deserts. All my life I have lived out many real stories in this country. This is a wonderful book that I found compulsive; it is a gem and is so readable it flows like a stream. It is a must for adventurers, domestic and foreign. It is a valuable guidebook to treasure after treasure. Each chapter is a new story. It will show you a variety of experiences that will give a breathtaking panorama of California, an essence of the land that is often missed. This book can also enhance your library or home for your guests.

Have fun and enjoy!

EMMETT HARDER
Author of *These Canyons Are Full of Ghosts:*
The Last of the Death Valley Prospectors

Emmett Harder.

Acknowledgements

We are indebted to C.R. King for his expertise in western history. He has authored three books: *The Last Deputy*, *A Fraternity of Gunslingers: True Stories of Wild West Gunmen* and *A Fraternity of Gunslingers: True Stories of Wild West Gunmen, Vol. 2*.

We thank Karen Garrett of Happy Camp and Pat De Rose of Duarte for their tedious work in proofreading our manuscript.

Our heartfelt thanks go to author, adventurer and historian Emmett Harder for writing the foreword to this book.

Since the opening of the West, desert characters have come and gone. But for those who relish desert history, their stories might have been forgotten. Salvation Mountain is an example of what a man can accomplish if he follows his heart. Upon his death, Leonard Knight's bizarre mountain would have crumbled. However, it survives today because of volunteers who see value in protecting desert art no matter the form. We thank the artists, the dreamers, the environmentalists, the quirky desert travelers and those who work to protect the offbeat places and characters described in this book.

Introduction

Follow the footsteps of the last great manhunt in California, visit ancient intaglios and contemplate their mystery or rejuvenate your inner self according to directions from an extraterrestrial! These adventures and many more await those who dare. Most are easily accessible and require a car, an imagination and the desire to escape everyday life.

For years, curious sites of the California deserts have beckoned inquiring minds to discover historical and quirky places that pique the imagination. Some are lessons in history while others present unanswered questions. These are adventures the entire family can enjoy together and emerge with educational and spiritual results.

Throughout history, miners, prospectors, lost souls and adventurers have been attracted to the desert and left their mark. Today, remnants of their presence are scattered about telling stories of obsession, creativity and resourcefulness. Geologic sites offer such exciting adventures as mud caves, strange natural formations and artwork created by lost civilizations. Ghost towns tug at the imagination with collapsed cabins, mining pits and rock-walled military encampments.

The deserts of California are designated as such because they are deprived of rain due to the rain-shadow effect. Deserts have unique ecosystems and offer dynamic natural features. Vast views of uncluttered land present respite from city life. Remnants of the old Wild West encourage visitors to study the past. Scenic sand dunes, rugged canyons and picturesque mesas and buttes are irresistible to photographers. Brilliant sunsets soothe the soul. Vast blue skies dotted with puffy snow-white clouds rise high above the desert floor while a multitude of critters scurry around above and below ground.

Most people refer to and are familiar with the Mojave Desert, which stretches from the Tehachapi Mountains and the Owens Valley to the northwest with the San Gabriel and San Bernardino Mountains to the south. It is the hottest of the California deserts, and although it is called the "high desert," it is most famous for Death Valley, which is the lowest elevation in North America. If surrounded by Joshua trees and creosote bushes, it is probable that you are in the Mojave Desert.

However, California boasts three deserts. The arid Sonoran Desert, sometimes referred to as the Colorado Desert, covers 127,000 miles in southwestern Arizona and southeastern California as well as most of Baja and some of Sonora Mexico. It is in this desert we find California's largest state park: Anza-Borrego and the nearby tourist haven of Palm Springs. This area is referred to as the low desert, where temperatures soar in the summer months.

Less known is the Great Basin Desert, often referred to as the cool desert because the rain-shadow effect cools the air that has passed over snow-covered mountains. It is the largest of the California deserts and is bordered by the Sierra Nevada Range on the west, the Rocky Mountains on the east, the Columbia Plateau on the north and the Mojave and Sonoran Deserts on the south.

Traveling through the desert, one might feel thousands of miles from civilization, yet what seems like a far-off land is usually only a short drive from some of the state's largest cities. Throughout these vast lands, there are oddities waiting to be discovered, some natural and others manmade. Although off-road vehicles take those in search of adventure into hard-to-reach places, many curious and historic sites are easily reached by passenger cars.

The National Park Service has been entrusted with the care of many areas of the deserts since 1916, but only in the year 1994 was the Mojave Preserve designated to protect 1.6 million square miles of desert in San Bernardino County between I-15 and I-40. It is home to the historic Mojave Road, the National Trails Highway and Route 66. Within its boundaries are a multitude of historic and natural sites to discover.

Some sites are touted in guidebooks while others are hidden from the public. Some are marked on maps while others are discovered by chance. Some are championed by environmentalists or history buffs and protected from further decay while others have melted into the ground and are barely discernible. Desert travel is fun and exciting, but some precautions are suggested.

INTRODUCTION

DESERT TRAVEL

It was a spontaneous decision to exit I-10 on our way home from Las Vegas. We had heard of the loneliest telephone booth in the world and wanted to check it out. With only a vague idea of where it was located, we took off on a dirt road in search. A short while later, I realized we had broken every rule of desert travel. No one knew where we were. We had little gas and less water. Our car tires were spinning in the deep sand, and this was before cellphones, which would not have had reception anyway. Fortunately, it was an exciting day that ended well and is described in detail later in this book.

Desert travel requires common sense as well as a car in good working condition, maps, food, a gallon a day per person of drinking water and a cellphone. Extreme temperatures are a definite concern for desert travelers. Summer rains can bring on flash floods where a tiny stream might become a raging river in a short amount of time. Desert dwellers are fun to spot from a distance. High-top hiking boots are the safest way to trek through the desert, even in the summer. Jumping cholla, snakes and red ants can cause damage to unprotected feet. Insect repellant is suggested. Sunblock and wide-brimmed hats serve as protection from the summer sun.

While exploring abandoned mines is a favorite desert pastime, tunnels can collapse and mines might harbor poisonous air. For this reason, the park service has closed off some mining areas and filled in tunnels and shafts. Avoid caves or shelters containing evidence of rodent droppings to avoid exposure to the hantavirus.

GETTING STARTED

After perusing the sites described, you probably will have flagged a list of destinations. All that is needed is a working car and some imagination and desire. Depending on where you live, some trips can be done in a day while others might take a few days to explore. Check the weather and pack food, water, maps and other necessities, not the least of which is a camera.

Desert exploration may take a bit of planning. However, it is free of airline costs, security lines and dealing with a foreign language. Although the world offers amazing historic sites and endless curiosities both manmade and natural, the California deserts are a haven of strange, unusual and peculiar places and things that are just as intriguing as those abroad. They tell the story of our history and geology. They are the treasures of our state and have been protected so that all of us can enjoy them. This, of course, is a reminder to never collect artifacts in the desert or on any public lands. These pieces of history belong where they lie, not in a box in someone's garage.

Getting There

You will note that this book does not offer exact directions to many of the sites described. Some are obvious, such as the giant thermometer in Baker. Others, like the Mojave Cross, are located on small desert roads. We believe the journey is as important and exciting as the destination. Some directions are loose and may require a bit of ingenuity while others have an actual address. You can find GPS coordinates on the Internet. When looking for an unusual site, you may find a previously undiscovered site of your own.

The Authors' Declaration

In this age of the Internet, it is possible and probably common that people write travel articles about places they have never visited and without ever leaving their office. The authors of this book feel confident that readers are able to ascertain whether a writer has actually experienced that which he or she writes about. Over the years, Alan and Claudia Heller have not only visited all of the sites described in this book but have returned to revisit them over and over. Most of the photographs were personally snapped by Alan Heller, some during the days of film photography that had to be developed and were not subject to "photoshopping."

PART I
Curiosities and Oddities

SALVATION MOUNTAIN AND SLAB CITY

The beauty of the desert partly lies in its subtle colors—the sandy dunes, the low-lying shrubs and miles of gravel and dirt punctuated with brilliant flowers on the short term. That is why after driving through the dilapidated town of Niland, it is a shock to see a most curious colorful site: Salvation Mountain.

The bright greens, reds and yellows against a blue desert sky confuse the senses, and it takes a while to comprehend this anomaly that is so out of place in a bland surrounding. The fifty-foot-high mountain fashioned with adobe, straw and discarded desert junk is painted the brightest of greens with a giant red heart at its center. Six-foot letters spell "LOVE," and a white cross rises to the sky from the mountaintop. It is obviously not an ancient Native American ritual site. Who would create such a bizarre shrine and why?

The "who" is a kind, quiet and passionate man who longed to show his love of God and man by creating this folk art masterpiece. His name is Leonard Knight, and his creation, which he began in 1985, constantly grew as he added rooms and caves and meandering paths. So dedicated was Leonard that he lived at the foot of the mountain, a life with no modern amenities such as electricity, sewage, running water or telephone. His "home" was built onto a 1939 white pickup truck that he had ornately decorated. Leonard's primitive lifestyle was a challenge in an area subject to

Featured on a *Huell Howser* episode, acting in the movie *Into the Wild* and recognized by Senator Barbara Boxer of California by way of proclamation, Leonard greeted thousands of visitors annually. His health began to decline in 2011, and after a few years in an assisted care facility, he died in February 2014. His mountain empire is, for the time, maintained by friends.

extreme temperatures most of the year and to a man in his senior years. He welcomed anyone who drove onto the property and was happy to show them around or just sit and talk for hours. He never charged a fee nor did he make an effort to convert visitors to any particular faith. He loved everyone and told them so.

As Leonard grew older, his hearing waned so he would strategically seat his guests under a tarp next to his truck in order to hear with his "good ear."

He would ask them to send out news and photos of his compound on that "whadda ya call it—innenet?" He would hand out postcards depicting his mountain, free of charge.

Leonard was particularly pleased with a plaque he received from Senator Barbara Boxer of California documenting a May 15, 2002 entry into the Congressional Record of the United States proclaiming Salvation Mountain as a national treasure. Boxer is quoted as describing Salvation Mountain as "a unique and visionary sculpture…a national treasure…profoundly strange and beautifully accessible, and worthy of the international acclaim it receives." The story of Salvation Mountain and its creator is the subject of a show on California Gold by the late Huell Howser. The mountain is also featured in the movie *Into the Wild* in which Leonard appeared, playing himself.

When Leonard's health further declined in December 2011, he was moved to an assisted care facility and later diagnosed with dementia. He died on February 10, 2014.

What is the future of Salvation Mountain? So loved by the many people Leonard befriended, the mountain is currently protected by a group of volunteers. Visitors donate money and paint needed to maintain the shrine, which is constantly bombarded by the elements of the desert. There was a time when Leonard was hard at work on his mountain that the powers that be threatened its existence because of "unacceptable amounts of lead in the paint." It was saved when tests were done showing that the lead content was at a legal mark. This and the fact that thousands protested any talk of closing the area seemingly has encouraged the local agencies to turn a blind eye.

Salvation Mountain is located in Imperial County just a few miles out of Niland, east of the Salton Sea. The address is listed simply as East Beal Road, Niland. Directions: North of I-8, south of I-10, five miles east of Highway 111 at Niland.

Nearby are other desert oddities, including "Slab City," which exists only yards from the mountain and, in nearby Calipatria, the "world's tallest flagpole," a claim that has now been demoted.

The people living in Slab City do not seem to mind visitors, especially ones who bring books for their library or clothes for those who need them.

When the World War II marine barracks were abandoned at Camp Dunlap, only the cement slabs remained. Since the 1950s, the area has become home to squatters, some of whom remain for years while others are dubbed "snowbirds," migrating from the east and staying only during the winter months.

This community is "decommissioned and uncontrolled" except for the rules imposed by those who live there. Many are seeking freedom from the confines of civilization. Some remain because they have no money and nowhere else to go. They live simply without modern conveniences such as electricity, running water, trash pickup, mail, sewers or toilets. Nearby hot springs are used for bathing. Some survive with solar panels or generators. Those living in RVs can drive the four miles to Niland to fetch water and other supplies. Some "dwellings" are but lean-tos that can be attached to a car, many of which are no longer in working order. Although this description may conjure up a sad scene, Slab City is not really a sad place.

The Slabbers, as they are called, police themselves and have established meeting places and even a library. Visitors drop off clothes and shoes for those who need them and sometimes even food. They have established an "official website" on which they have indicated their biggest problem: trash. With no organized trash pickup in the area, piles accumulate.

The community of Slab City is also described as a weird town filled with druggies, hippies and those too strange to live in a city. But it is also called "the last free place to live in America." The inhabitants do not own the land, and it seems the government has chosen not to look their way. That is perhaps the reason they police themselves so as to not call too much attention to their lifestyle.

Like in any neighborhood, driving through, you will notice the neat camps, the manicured areas and the areas that are unsightly and filled with junk. There also seems to be an artistic flair where gardens of hubcaps or desert junk adorn the camps. The sign outside the area proudly announces, "Slab City."

Slab City is truly an oddity in the desert. These refugees from city life live peacefully for the most part. There are old-timers who have made their home on the slabs for years, and there are transients and snowbirds. It is interesting to drive through this odd place and see how the "free people" live.

To reach Slab City, follow the directions to Salvation Mountain above and continue past the mountain. Slab City is just beyond.

Giant Rock and Integratron

Some of the most exciting and accessible oddities of the Mojave Desert are to be found in Landers, an unincorporated town of about 2,500 people in San Bernardino County. This area was the epicenter of the 1992 Landers earthquake, a magnitude of 7.3. With an extraterrestrial flair, exploring

Giant Rock, the alien landing strip and the incomparable Integratron is a true adventure. The odd story of this area's history renders it one of the most bizarre places in the desert.

Giant Rock

"Darn! It's huge!" is the common phrase exclaimed upon beholding Giant Rock for the first time. The boulder stands about seven stories high and was revered by Native Americans long before white men appeared. Thought to be the world's largest freestanding boulder, Giant Rock's intrigue goes far beyond its geological traits. Its history is remarkable and quite difficult to believe.

Modern history of the rock began in the early 1930s when German immigrant Frank Critzer, a prospector who carried a curmudgeonly reputation topped off with a mean streak, arrived on the scene. People avoided him when possible. Armed with squatter's rights and a mining claim, Critzer burrowed under Giant Rock and built a "home." There he could remain sheltered from the extreme heat of the desert and pursue his passion, which focused on his short-wave radio. For reception, he attached a radio antenna to the top of the rock.

It was by chance that Critzer made acquaintance with George Van Tassel, who arrived at Giant Rock on his invitation. George will enter the picture again later in this story.

Life for Critzer became difficult as World War II started. The authorities became suspicious of his activities based on the fact that he was German, holed up under a boulder and kept his short-wave radio in use constantly. He had also established a landing strip nearby. The "spying" rumor spread, causing three FBI agents to check out the strange scenario. As usual, Critzer greeted them in his confrontational way, so things did not start out well. Not as clueless as he might have seemed, Critzer knew these agents had no authority as they were from Riverside County, and Landers is in San Bernardino County. He was, to the say the least, uncooperative.

The story goes that Critzer barricaded himself in his subterranean home, defying the demands of the agents to come out. In frustration, the agents attempted to smoke him out by tossing a tear gas grenade into his abode. The device landed on a pack of dynamite that Critzer had stashed. After the explosion, Critzer lay dead, and the agents suffered injuries.

The Alien Landing Strip

After Critzer's demise, Van Tassel returned to the area as a permanent resident, reopened the landing field that Critzer had constructed and established a café there. He was a renowned pilot and gained a reputation as a test pilot during the war. After leasing the land around Giant Rock, he brought his family to the area. The rumor is that Van Tassel became friends with Howard Hughes during the war and that Hughes would fly into the Giant Rock area to dine at the café.

Van Tassel began hosting UFO conventions at the site, a project that brought him enough donations to support his family. Thousands of "believers" were drawn to the area, and in 1959, the UFO convention purportedly attracted more than eleven thousand people.

His café, conventions and family kept Van Tassel busy, but he found time to work on his true dream, which was to build the Integratron. This would fit right into the subject of his many writings on the subjects of rejuvenation and time travel. It is said that while meditating under Giant Rock, Van Tassel received information from extraterrestrials as to how he should build the Integratron. The location of this dome was of utmost importance due to many factors, not the least of which was its relationship to Giant Rock and to the Great Pyramid of Egypt. The magical spot just happened to be only a few miles from the rock. He gained many followers who believed that this "machine" would rejuvenate human cells.

The Integratron History

Together with his brother, Jack, and donations from his followers, Van Tassel began construction of the Integratron in 1953, a two-story domed building constructed of concrete and wood and containing no metal. It is said to be "acoustically perfect." The structure contains sixteen glued and laminated spines held together at its apex with a ton of concrete. His plan was designed by "aliens from Venus" and built on a vortex of energy.

Van Tassel's dream had come true. His Integratron was built to recharge energy in living cells and bring about longer life. He gained a worldwide reputation, wrote books about alien travel and lectured to his followers. During the 1960s and '70s, Van Tassel enjoyed celebrity status and was in full swing of his dream when he died of a heart attack. His family was at a loss, with no clue of how the Integratron worked or

Born out of George Van Tassell's lifelong dream and furthered by his collaboration with extraterrestrials, the Integratron was born. A two-story dome constructed with no metal is deemed to be acoustically perfect and is home to the signatory sound bath that recharges energy into living cells to bring about a longer life. It is today available to the public.

what was to be done next. They abandoned the project. The buildings at Giant Rock were also abandoned and eventually destroyed and hauled off by the Bureau of Land Management.

The Integratron Today

The Integratron stands today, visited by people from all over the world to tour and partake in its signature sound bath. Occasional UFO conventions are held, and it is a popular site for renting and for filming movies. For the past twenty-five years, it has been owned by three sisters who have diligently tended to its maintenance and preservation. For the first time, it is open to the public.

The sound bath experience is explained as a "kindergarten naptime for adults" and consists of a session of deep relaxation in the upstairs room of the dome. Reclined on mats, patrons are treated to a sixty-minute sonic healing session. The first twenty minutes consist of the sounds of vibrating quartz crystal singing bowls skillfully played, each one keyed to the energy centers of the body. The balance of the hour is to "integrate the sound and relax in the sound chamber to recorded music resulting in waves of peace, heightened awareness and relaxation of the mind and body."

It is suggested that a reservation be made to be sure the compound will be open. The Integratron is located at 2477 Belfield Boulevard, Landers, California, 92285.

Giant Rock and the alien landing field are located north of Landers near the Integratron.

The Giant Intaglios of Blythe

The awesome sight of a giant etching of a man spread out across an area of the upper Sonoran Desert near Blythe, California, stimulates the imagination and begs the obvious question: why?

This giant intaglio near Blythe depicts a bigger-than-life man. And like his neighboring intaglios, his form is better understood from space. Who created him? Who is he there to impress? A visitor leaves with more questions than answers!

Known as the Blythe Intaglios or geoglyphs, an odd collection of intaglios has been preserved with fences and is open to the public. Walk among them and you, too, may leave asking many questions and gaining few answers. The human figure measures 105.6 feet. Nearby lies an animal about half that size and then a spiral, or maze, about 26.0 feet in length.

To understand what is there, the word intaglio is the key. It simply means "etching." Over the years, as the desert sun bakes the top layer of rocks, the rocks take on a dark color called desert varnish. The rocks and soil below remain a lighter color, as the sun's rays do not reach them. Scraping away the dark rock to reveal the lighter can make it possible to draw pictures on the desert floor. Although this may answer the "how" question, the probing query remains: who did this, and why?

The answers are elusive but not without thoughtful guesses by scientists and laypersons. Four hundred to ten thousand years ago seems to be the popular guess as to when they were created. They are so large that it is hard to decipher the forms from the ground. Could it be they were not discovered until man invented airplanes and flew above the area? The story goes that a pilot, George Palmer, flew over these intaglios in 1931. This creates another puzzle: why would those who created these characters make them so big as to only be deciphered from space? For some, the answer is simple: alien visitors. To others, this explanation is outrageous.

As to the "who" question, it is believed that the intaglios were created by ancestors of today's Native Americans living along the Colorado River. Perhaps the drawings are messages to their gods or ancestors

Walking among these giant desert drawings presents an intriguing mystery. Discover the giant man as well as several other figures in addition to a labyrinth that is guessed to be ceremonial in nature.

There are dozens of intaglios throughout the deserts of California and Arizona. Some intaglio hunters are so passionate about visiting them all that they rent planes and pilots and fly over these areas for an optimum view.

In addition, the California etchings are reminiscent of the famous Nazca lines and giant ground drawings that appear across thirty miles of gravel-covered desert near Peru's southern coast. Discovered in 1982, they are referred to as "Riddles in the Sand."

Directions to the Blythe Intaglios: from I-10, exit onto U.S. 95/Intake Boulevard just west of the California-Arizona state line. Travel 15.5 miles on U.S. 95. At the right is a small stone cairn, and on the left is a fenced dirt road that leads to the intaglios.

Burro Schmidt's Tunnel: Obsession or Folly?

For thirty-eight years, Burro Schmidt painstakingly dug his tunnel armed with a pick, shovel and hammer. Day in and day out, Schmidt moved rock and soil until he broke through to the far side of the mountain. Then he left, never to return.

To walk through the tunnel today is to reflect on history and the plight of old-time prospectors who faced daunting challenges to be met with crude tools and extreme conditions. Straddling the tracks and sometimes bending slightly, visitors feel relief as the light at the end of the tunnel comes into view. Why did Schmidt obsess with completing his tunnel and then turn his back on it?

It was the year 1900 when Schmidt was mining gold near the summit of a 4,400-foot mountain in the El Paso Mountains near Last Chance Canyon.

Schmidt's story begins as many others did at that time. Diagnosed with a respiratory ailment, he was advised to move to a dry climate, and the Mojave Desert fit the bill. He traveled from his home in Rhode Island, arriving in Bakersfield in the late 1890s. Hearing that gold had been discovered in the El Paso Mountains, he struck out to make his fortune. Accompanied by Jenny and Jack, his two burros, he staked his claims.

Mining the claims, it didn't take long for Schmidt to realize that hauling thousands of tons of rock to the smelter located in Mojave on the other side of the mountain would be an almost impossible achievement for him to accomplish alone. He thought of a much better option: dig a tunnel through the mountain through which to haul the rock. He began to dig—and dig and dig.

While boring his tunnel, Schmidt lived in a crude one-room cabin, the inside of which was plastered with newspaper pages. It is said that one could learn about history-making events of those days by reading the many headlines, one of which made reference to the famed kidnapping and murder of Charles Lindbergh's baby. A cast-iron stove served for cooking simple meals as well as providing a source of heat.

In the year 1900, Schmidt began his life's work of burrowing through solid granite using crude tools and short-fused dynamite. Often injured by falling rock and flying particles, he was lucky to live through the ordeal. Schmidt was a determined man, and eventually, he made life a little easier by installing an oar cart on rails. During the hottest months of the year, he would abandon his project to hire out as a ranch hand, using his wages to fund his mining operation.

It is said that while excavating his tunnel, Schmidt hit some gold veins, but by that time, he was so obsessed with completing the tunnel he apparently did not notice them or was just too busy to bother with them. His mind was as one-tracked as his tunnel. However, it has also been said that he was aware of the gold veins in his tunnel but chose not to tell anyone, hiding his motives behind digging the tunnel. During these excavation years, a road was built that he could have utilized, but by that time, he was hell-bent on finishing the tunnel. *Ripley's Believe it or Not!* branded him "the human mole."

At the conclusion of his project, Schmidt deeded his mine and tunnel to a friend and walked away. A plaque located seventeen miles south of Randsburg in the Mojave Desert was erected by the Ancient and Honorable Order of E Clampus Vitus. It reads:

Burro Schmidt began his excavation task with crude tools and short-fused dynamite. Eventually he installed a track, removing the debris with an oar cart. The tracks remain today.

> *A monument to determination and perseverance. William Henry "Burro" Schmidt took thirty-eight years to hand-dig this half-mile long tunnel completed in 1938. Born in Rhode Island, January 30, 1871—died in Ridgecrest Calif., January 27, 1954. And So Recorded, May 16, 1970, E Clampus Vitus, Peter Lebeck Chapter 1866.*

Word of the tunnel and its creator traveled, resulting in visitors anxious to see the fruits of Schmidt's labors. A walk through the tunnel was thought to be a sort of rite of passage. After Schmidt abandoned the area, an old friend named Mike Lee led tours through the tunnel until his death in 1963. After that, people came and went, occupying cabins in the area and serving as caretakers.

After Schmidt's Death

In 1963, the rights to the tunnel were awarded through probate court to Milo and Evelyn Seger for the sum of $5,000. Shortly after moving to the area from Huntington Park, Milo died. Evelyn, who preferred to be called "Tonie," remained, leading tours through the tunnel for the many visitors. She died in 2003 after living for forty years in a five-room cabin, only yards from the famed tunnel.

The Cabin and Tunnel Today

The compound is now on federal land maintained by the Bureau of Land Management. In an effort to protect the cabins from vandalism, the structures have been fenced. It is worth a visit to the area for the breathtaking desert views and, of course, a trek through the infamous tunnel. At one time, a caretaker would offer visitors the use of a lantern, but that is a hit-or-miss proposition today. Visitors should be equipped with a flashlight, sturdy shoes and drinking water. The tunnel trek takes about thirty minutes as you straddle the oar car tracks and head for the light at the end.

A two-seater outhouse also stands on the property, and although there is a lack of privacy with no door, it faces the vast desert beyond and offers a great view.

To reach Burro Schmidt's tunnel and cabins, take Highway 14. Not too far north of Red Rock Canyon State Park, there is a cluster of large billboards, and that is where the tunnel road turns east.

THE GIANT THERMOMETER OF BAKER

While some people dream of winning the lottery, Willis Herron dreamed of building the world's biggest thermometer. Maybe this makes sense since he lived in Baker, California, the gateway to Death Valley, where temperatures are extreme. Indeed, his dream came true, and the 125-foot-high thermometer was constructed next to Herron's Bun Boy Restaurant at a cost of $700,000, not to mention the $8,000-a-month electric bill. The thermometer is said to have topped off at 127 degrees in August 1995.

The giant thermometer of Baker stands at 125 feet, cost more than $700,000 to construct and rakes up an electrical bill of $8,000 monthly. It topped off at 127 degrees in August 1995. The monstrosity is visible from nearby I-15.

Constructed in 1990, the thermometer is visible from the nearby I-15 and soon became recognized as an oddity of the desert. However, extreme weather in Baker includes high winds, which partially toppled the monstrosity in 1992. Herron's dream continued after rebuilding his thermometer where it remained for many years with no rivals worldwide. Herron died in 1997, and although the monument continued for a time, it stopped working in 2012. The new owners balked at the cost of repair.

But family ties are strong, and along came Herron's daughter, who bought the thermometer. With family help, the thermometer was again repaired and has been working since October 2014. A gift shop was established at its base.

Directions to the thermometer are not necessary because it is so visible. However, the address is 72157 Baker Boulevard in Baker, California.

The Curious Desert View Tower

There are many odd things about the Desert View Tower and its location. Sitting just off I-8 in San Diego County, the closest towns are Jacumba and Ocotillo. The area is within the In-Koh-Pa mountain range. On the way, visitors will pass "Coyote's Flying Saucer Retrievals and Repairs—Service," a service station for space ships. With your imagination already piqued, arrive at the stone lookout known as the Desert View Tower, and you will realize you are confronting something bizarre.

The seventy-foot-high tower is an imposing sight against the bluest of desert skies and begs the question: what the heck is this place?

The owner of the town of Jacumba, Bert Vaughn, built the tower, which he completed in 1923. His aim was to commemorate the area's use by those traveling from the east and west, including explorers, pioneers, railway workers and quirky desert wanderers. He also dedicated the tower to the many trails and roads crossing through the area. Among these primitive roads was the "old plank road," sections of which jut from the walls of the tower. For centuries, travelers passed through this area, many leaving their marks. Vaughn wanted to honor the builders of the railway and the more modern highways that made traveling safer and easier.

In 1947, Dennis Newman bought the tower from the Vaughns and added the round lower floor in 1950. Today, it is known as the last functioning roadside attraction on the San Diego–Yuma corridor.

The tower is flanked by an earth flag, and after entering, you may wonder if you have invaded someone's home. Comfortable couches and chairs invite you to sit for a while, but that won't happen because there is too much to see by way of souvenirs, Native American artifacts, vintage photos, bizarre books, cards and bumper stickers. Don't trip over the sleeping dogs and cats.

A climb to the top of the tower by way of stairs is rewarded with an endless view of the Imperial Valley and the Anza-Borrego Desert.

Just yards from the tower sits a canyon of granite boulders known as Boulder Park. This fantasy canyon is an easy climb, and along the way you will be accompanied by stone-carved statues of a variety of creatures created by W.T. Ratliffe. So intriguing and unique are these statues that the canyon is one of California's exceptional folk art environments designated as California Registered Historical Landmark No. 939.

The Desert View Tower, Boulder Canyon and surrounding outbuildings featuring colorful murals are open to the public seven days a week. There is a small fee to enter the tower and explore the area.

The Desert View Tower stands at a cool three thousand feet above sea level, three miles east of Jacumba, on the north side of I-8 at the In-Ko-Pah Road exit. Billboards point the way.

CABOT YERXA AND HIS PUEBLO

Climb the dusty stairs and peek into the cubbies and out the windows. Visiting the pueblo of Cabot Yerxa is to go back in time and to get to know one of the desert's most colorful and respected adventurers.

Known as a true explorer, visionary, intellect, champion of human rights, collector and architect, Cabot ultimately settled in the Desert Hot Springs area after years of wandering through Alaska and Mexico. He spent time traveling abroad and studied in Paris at the Academie Julian. What drew this man to the California desert?

After Cabot's family lost their fortune in a California citrus industry frost, he headed to the desert. In 1930, at age thirty-two, Cabot homesteaded 188 acres in a lonely patch of desert that is now part of a housing community and designated as 67616 East Desert View Avenue, Desert Hot Springs, California, 92240. After meeting a local Indian who showed him where water could be found, he went in search. Poking around the area, he took up a pick and shovel and dug. He was surprised to hit water that was hot! At a nearby location, he again dug into the earth and was just as surprised to hit water that was cold. What better place to build a homestead? Soon, the land on which his homestead stood became known as Miracle Hill. Cabot always believed that this was sacred land.

Cabot built his abode in the Coachella Valley between 1941 and 1950. It became his home and personal museum until his death in 1965. His pueblo encompassed a museum in which he displayed items collected from his travels, his collection of Native American crafts and his own paintings. Visitors would be treated to his personal stories. Cabot became known as one of the fathers of Desert Hot Springs. He loved to explore his lands accompanied by his burro, Merry Christmas.

Before taking off to serve in the army in World War I, Cabot built a structure that had one window and one door and was mostly underground. He called it Eagle's Nest. Returning from the war, he found his Eagle's Nest nearly destroyed by vandals. He began to build what is called today Cabot's Pueblo Museum. Current tours meet in the Desert Hot Springs Water Gallery, where displays show the geology of the area, the San Andreas Earthquake Fault and facts about the "healing waters."

Narrow dusty staircases on packed dirt and recycled lumber scaffolding wind through the four-story building, which contains 150 windows and 65 doors, no two of which are alike. The architecture is Hopi style. It is said that the lumber is recycled and the poles retrieved from mountain floods. Cabot let nothing go to waste, straightening out bent nails to re-use. Air conditioning is by way of the venturi effect. The tour winds through Cabot's office, a small kitchen, sitting room and entertainment room with piano, bedrooms and bath. He made sure his wife, Portia, always had both hot and cold running water. Artwork by Cabot and that of his friends hang on the walls, as well as curios and relics from his travels. Tours through the home are limited to about twelve participants, and tickets are on a first-come, first-served basis. Tours last about forty-five to sixty minutes.

Cabot died in 1965 at his home at the age of eighty-one, and his pueblo fell into disrepair. It would have been lost but for Cole Eyraud, who moved in and carried on the traditions that Cabot had established. Cole carried on for twenty-six years, and in 1998, after his death, the compound was donated to the City of Desert Hot Springs. The museum grounds seem to exude a mystical aura. The unusual architecture, the reverence for the man who built it and the quiet surroundings, which Cabot dedicated to the Hopi, seem to capture the souls of those who meander through the area.

On the hill behind the museum is Waokiye, a forty-three-foot-tall carving of a feathered Indian that was carved of sequoia and cedar by Peter Wolf Toth in 1978. Toth has created at least one monument in each state, two in Canada and one in his birthplace of Hungary, a project he termed the "Trail of the Whispering Giants." His artwork is intended to raise awareness of the spirit, culture and plight of the Native Americans.

Also on the grounds is the Wilderness Meditation Garden, which was dedicated in 1952. Cabot envisioned it as a place where "each person might, in his or her own way, visit the shrine to quietly meditate, read or pray and obtain a spiritual uplift of thought." After his death, an altar was erected in the garden by Eyraud.

In the 1970s, the structure stood out in the midst of vast wild lands that had not yet been exploited. Today, it continues to stand out, though surrounded by homes and schools and businesses. It is a tribute to the City of Desert Hot Springs and the countless volunteers who staff this unique homestead that it remains with us today and is in the National Register of Historic Places.

Tour times and other information can be found at the museum's website: www.CabotsMuseum.org.

THE MYSTIC MAZE

The Mystic Maze, also called the Topock Maze, is a bit difficult to explain, but when you see it, the mind will focus on its delicate beauty and you may inherently understand. It is oddly beautiful in a subtle way.

Located near Needles, California, it was a sacred site for the AhaMakav warriors, who would pause there for purification when returning home from battle. More than six hundred years old, this geoglyph consists of intricate patterns and paths that today's Native Americans in the area believe are part of a spiritual portal to the next life. Here, the bad souls become lost in the maze while good souls find their portal to the afterlife.

The Mystic Maze is not a true maze but rather a series of windrows created with geological features. It is said that the maze covered much more land at one time, but much of it was destroyed when the highway was built. It was first desecrated in the 1880s by the laying of tracks for the Southern Pacific Railroad. Roads and paths during the construction further destroyed parts of the maze. That construction is said to have destroyed a geoglyph

The subtlety of the Topock Maze, also called the Mystic Maze, located near Needles, tugs at the imagination. This series of "windrows" is believed to be a Native American spiritual portal to the next life.

of a human figure holding a snake. The sacred ambience of the area is further compromised as it is dissected by a major highway and is also the site of the PG&E compressor and treatment center. Still, after such disrespectful treatment, a portion remains and is now protected. A plaque at the viewpoint reads:

> *Here, upon this land where you now stand, is the Topock Maze; indeed, a cultural site of much importance to the tribe. To this site the AhaMakav warriors returning home from battle first paused for purification before continuing home.*
>
> *Not a true maze, this site is a series of windrows carefully placed in an extensive geometric pattern. Today, the site covers about 10 acres. Evidence suggests that it may have originally been only one section in a group of nearby earth images and features. Sadly, important parts of the complex were destroyed by the construction of the highway. But whether or not the geoglyphs in this vicinity were associated with one another, this was clearly an area of symbolic and ritual significance.*

In 1978, the Topock Maze was added to the National Register of Historic Places.

To reach the maze, exit at Park Moabi Road off I-40 and go south. Follow the pavement until it ends, and turn left onto a well-maintained and graded road. Continue about one mile. The maze will be on the north (left) side of the road in a fenced-in area.

DEVILS HOLE AND THE PLIGHT OF THE DESERT PUPFISH

The plight of the desert pupfish resembles a rollercoaster ride, and chances are the ending won't be very pretty.

Why does this odd little fish attract such a large crowd of followers? Maybe because it is just an example of what man has done to destroy what it cannot use or sell. The pupfish has fought a mighty battle, from which we can learn. These tenacious desert fish live in a spring known as Devils Hole.

By way of history, the pupfish we are talking about is only one species of this type of fish. At one time, Lake Manly covered the floor of Death Valley, and these perky little pupfish enjoyed a unique habitat, swam freely and

Fenced and protected, the site of Devils Hole in Death Valley appears sterile and untouchable. However, it houses a delicate species of fish that has all but disappeared and is reportedly hanging on by its pectorals.

A group of members of the National Speleological Society visit Devils Hole for a work project, circa 1950. *Courtesy of the archives of the NSS.*

thrived. In time, the lake dried up, and the pupfish could only survive by clinging to the springheads that remained. Because of the widely different ecological circumstances of the individual springheads, the fish speciated, each school adapting to the ecological circumstances of the springhead at which it lived. One group clung to a spring called Devils Hole and were thus classified as the Devils Hole Pupfish, or *Cyprinodon diabolis*.

Devils Hole and nearby Ash Meadows are located a slip over the California border in Nevada. Although not physically attached, they are an annex to Death Valley National Park by declaration of President Truman in 1952. In 1963, the Devils Hole pupfish was officially listed as endangered and was on the very first official listing of endangered species in 1970. There were about 550 individuals counted at that time. Later, its relative the Warm Springs Pupfish was added.

It is said that Devils Hole is a perfect habitat, so why is the fish threatened? The actions of mankind have set out to destroy these fish. Their home is a water-filled cavern deemed to be bottomless. Divers have explored to three hundred feet and were unable to find an end. Indeed, divers have attempted to follow the cavern to greater depths only to disappear and never be found. Just below the surface is a feeding shelf where algae grows, and it is that algae on which the fish survive. Because the water surface is located yards below the desert floor, sun reaches the feeding ledge only a few hours a day.

In the 1960s, ranches were established in the area, resulting in the pumping of groundwater, which caused the water level in Devils Hole to recede. When the surface falls below the feeding ledge, the fish are unable to feed. With the area growing, plans were on the drawing board for additional ranches, farms and housing developments. Could these little fish fight progress? Amazingly, with the help of the "Save the Pupfish" movement, this is an environmental fight that was ultimately successful. Those who believe it is not up to man to wipe out any living thing declared war, and the courts stepped in. The Department of Justice filed a complaint, and some of the major wells ceased pumping. However, water levels in the hole continued to decline, and in 1976, the United States Supreme Court limited water pumping in the area. The surrounding land was up for sale, and there was talk of vast housing projects and the building of a "mini city." It was then that the Nature Conservancy purchased the land and later sold it to the U.S. Department of Fish and Wildlife. The area known as Ash Meadows officially became a refuge in 1984.

Devils Hole is a popular spot for tourists to visit. A short trek up a hill offers a partial view of the hole, which is surrounded by a barbwire fence. Through the fence, you can peer down into the hole and view the water surface and the feeding ledge. Strewn about the area are various devices designed to measure the water level and emit a signal when the water recedes to a dangerous point.

Ash Meadows Natural Wildlife Refuge

The grand opening of this refuge and visitors' center was held in March 2015, and it is now open to the public. The facility offers an opportunity to learn about the ecological importance of the area and explains why it is protected. Exhibits explain the story behind the charismatic little pupfish, which resemble puppies playing as they dart to and fro in their hole. A small store sells books, brochures and souvenir items.

The refuge brochure sets forth the reasons behind its existence and explains what it offers to visitors:

> *Top reasons to visit Ash Meadows National Wildlife Refuge!*
> *1. It's the largest remaining oasis in the Mojave Desert.*

2. Nearly 30 species of plants and animals that do not exist anyplace else on earth (referred to as endemic species).

3. Ash Meadows has the highest concentration of endemic species in the United States.

4. See relict species of desert fish that have existed here since mammoths drank from these very springs.

5. Have you ever heard of fossil water? The water here is known as fossil water because it comes from melted ice from the last ice age.

6. This is a photographer's paradise where ice blue spring pools are a stark contrast against the harsh desert landscape.

7. Ash Meadows is recognized internationally as an important wetland.

8. The mysterious Devils Hole [is] over 500 feet deep and the bottom has never been found.

9. Each of the three boardwalks offers something unique to see and all are wheelchair accessible. There are picnic areas and benches too.

The area is open year round. Fall offers brilliant colors and the appearance of migrating birds while winter becomes a quiet and stark time. Spring finds Ash Meadows bursting with colors as wildflowers bloom, and summer sizzles with temperatures often soaring above the one-hundred-degree mark.

The Point of Rocks Boardwalk traverses a 0.07-mile round trip along crystal clear spring waters while the Crystal Springs Boardwalk, about the same length, offers spectacular views and interpretive signs along the way. In the blue and green spring waters you may spot the endearing little pupfish at play.

A visit to Ash Meadows and Devils Hole expands the Death Valley experience to a new level. The valley teems with curiosities that do not stop at its physical borders. The address is 610 East Spring Meadows Road, Amargosa Valley, Nevada, 89020.

An Intimate Encounter with a Devils Hole Pupfish

Following is an account of a personal experience with the charismatic pupfish. Photographer Alan Heller recalls his adventures in 1974 when he entered that bottomless hole to photograph this endangered fish. Invited to accompany a group of divers who were assigned the task of conducting a fish count, Alan snapped dozens of shots using a Nikonos underwater camera, one of the first underwater-type cameras that did not require a housing. In the cave, he used the old-style glass flashbulbs, as he was unable to afford the newly designed strobes. This was one of the first times the Devils Hole pupfish was photographed in its natural habitat.

"We've just come closer to hell than most people," remarked Art Partin, South District ranger of Death Valley National Monument as he emerged from what is probably one of the most unique and interesting dives in the Western United States.

Devils Hole, a desert spring located along Highway 137, seventy miles southwest of Las Vegas and three hundred miles from Los Angeles, is the largest opening to a huge underground water system in the sparse Nevada desert. A constant ninety-two degrees, the crystal-clear waters have been likened to those found in Northern Nevada, a convincing indication of the monumental underground water system believed to exist.

Not only is the spring itself unique, located in some of the most arid land in the United States, but living in its upper portions, and as far down as seventy-five feet, is a curious and one-of-a-kind creature which scientists call Cyprinodon diabolis. *More commonly referred to as the "desert pupfish," this unusual critter is the distant relative of a type of fish found in this area thousands of years ago at a time when this land was covered with lakes and streams. Although there are still other related species found in the surrounding areas,* Cyprinodon diabolis *of Devils Hole is the last of its kind and is literally holding on by its pectorals. Due to the encroachment of man in the area and the pumping of groundwater for cattle, the desert pupfish are barely holding their own on the growing list of endangered species.*

Securing permission to dive in Devils Hole is difficult because of its ecological importance and the fact that it is a rather dangerous place to dive. Over the years, at least three divers have been overwhelmed by its captivating serenity, and they have yet to be found. As of now, Devils Hole is considered to be bottomless. Searching divers have penetrated two hundred feet and with their lights could see the cave continuing on beneath them.

Being an amateur naturalist, underwater photographer, enthusiastic diver and spelunker (NSS member) and an unyielding fan of the desert pupfish, I was granted permission to enter the spring to record the behavior of the desert pupfish on film to grace the park files.

On a windy morning in February, I met Art and Clifford "Rocky" McCreight (Death Valley park ranger) at the small town of Death Valley Junction, and after a cup of coffee at the local café, we were off across the desert. Cattle grazing behind fences, shiny new grain and water tanks, and freshly traveled roads endlessly crisscrossing the desert floor were all conspicuous reminders of man's presence in the area.

As we approached a small canyon at the northeast portion of the valley, I could make out a fenced area, and I knew we had arrived. Anxiously, I approached the observation platform for my first glimpse of this most unique fish and its habitat. As I looked downward into the cleft in the earth, I thought immediately this was truly a "hole in the ground." As for the "Devil" part, that would remain to be seen. As I gazed into the opening, I could make out at the bottom a dark rectangular pool of water about thirty feet long and seven feet wide. It was cluttered with various pieces of measuring and recording equipment. To the casual pupfish admirer, the scene visible from the observation platform would be grossly disappointing after traveling three hundred miles from Los Angeles. However, my journey was to be amply rewarded, and with a sign from Art, we began to unload our dive gear.

Carrying gear through the gate and down a precarious ladder to a spot near the water took several trips, but by noon we were ready. We suited up quickly, knowing that the warm waters would be our only relief from the chill of the desert winds racing around us.

Wet suits, as well as weight belts, were not needed—only basic scuba equipment and a good source of light. After suiting up, we climbed down to the water's edge and across a plank bridge which protects the shallow portion where the majority of the pupfish feed and reproduce. It is this section of the habitat that is in danger of a receding water level due to indiscriminate pumping of wells in the area which could spell doom for the small inhabitants. The entrance area is small, as most of the surface is either a highly delicate feeding area or covered with water level measuring equipment. One at a time, we eased into the water where the shallow portion drops off into deeper water. It was great—ninety-two degrees has got to be the best—just like a bathtub and clear, at least one hundred feet or more visibility.

With masks in place and the final signal given, we slid beneath the surface. I followed the invading sun rays downward for my first glimpse of this strange world. Directly beneath me I made out a ledge and another at the edge of the darkness; the cave took on new proportions. It was long and narrow at this point, about seven feet by one hundred feet, like a crack or fault. The walls were white limestone with a smooth, lumpy appearance. Scattered around and wedged into the smaller crevices were various size boulders. It occurred to me that the ones overhead could dislodge at any moment. Also, on the sloping ledge, an old measuring device lay rusting,

Park rangers have held fish counts over the years. In 1974, divers once again entered the ninety-two-degree waters and were pleased with the numbers they found. Today, the desert pupfish are highly endangered and near extinction.

a curious item for wandering pupfish who may explore to this depth. At the fifty-foot level, the bottom slopes gradually downward to a point called "anvil rock" at seventy-five feet. From here, a tunnel about twenty feet in diameter continued steeply into the earth to undetermined depths. Into this passageway we continued to a depth of about eighty-five feet. Rocky stopped and tilted his light upward into what appeared to be a side passage. Later, topside, he informed me that it led to a subterranean room with an air pocket which he referred to as "Brown's Room." (Author's note: In a subsequent dive, I was able to enter and explore this room.)

After the exciting tour, we returned to the shallower portion of the cave where I proceeded to photograph this eerie world's primary inhabitant. Strobe lights were not yet popular, and taking photos with flashbulbs underwater was problematical. Pupfish have been spotted as deep as anvil rock, but only on occasion. Generally, they patronize the shallow ledge at the surface, with some browsing down to fifty feet. I did most of my work at the fifteen-foot level, where available light was sufficient to follow my quarry. It was also easier to maneuver here on the shallow ledge at the surface.

The pupfish, about one inch in length, are the smallest of the species in the area. Not a bit coy, they posed for me unblushingly, and I went about my photography work completely at ease and comfortable in such an ideal temperature.

After two hours in the water, I returned to the desert world above and found that the unyielding desert winds still whipped unmercifully. As I drove homeward, my thoughts returned to those persistent pupfish, now my intimate friends, and I tried to imagine what miraculous instincts they must possess which enabled them to survive for thousands of years under the most demanding of environmental changes. What could be the purpose of their unlikely survival only to find themselves today existing in a speck of the desert vastness at the mercy of man?

ANZA-BORREGO'S MANY CURIOSITIES

When eighteenth-century Spanish explorer Juan Bautista de Anza trekked through what is now Anza-Borrego State Park, did he make note of the oddities he encountered? If he blazed his way through the area today, he would probably not believe the sights he would see.

Anza-Borrego is the largest state park in California and is found in the Colorado Desert to the west of the Salton Sea and east of San Diego. It is so unlike what we think of as San Diego that the San Diego County signs look misplaced. A few oddities of this vast desert park include endearing metal sculptures, a ribbon of mud caves and curious trees. Those who explore this area just might spot an endangered bighorn sheep, a definite thrill.

Dragons and Dinosaurs

Probably the most curious of the bizarre but addicting sights in this park is the Sky Art, behind which is an odd story.

Start with an artist whose drive and wild imagination are equaled by his charismatic personality and desire to make his mother proud. Enter a millionaire who owns acres of land in the unincorporated town of Borrego Springs, which is surrounded by the state park. A series of events set forth in a book entitled *Ricardo Breceda: Accidental Artist* has resulted in a fascinating experience for those who seek out Breceda's brilliant artwork.

Rising to the sky from the desert sands of Gallata Meadows in Borrego Springs are the great sculptures artist Ricardo Breceda created for a project called Sky Art. More than 130 sculptures entice travelers to spend time with them and perhaps reflect on the many animals that once inhabited the area.

His sculptures are often quirky. Many depict animals that once inhabited the area, but some of the favorites are laced with fantasy. It is perhaps that aspect that makes them so endearing. Tourists are able to drive right up to the artwork and, if they wish, set up a tent and stay three days. Feel the metal, imagine the history and photograph to your heart's content. Sit and stay awhile.

Of the 130-plus sculptures, one in particular seems to stand out: a 350-foot-long dragon with a sea serpent body that undulates below and above the sandy desert, slithering beneath the road and finally erupting through the desert sand with the tail of a rattlesnake. The flaring horns and tentacles sweeping from the dragon's head are terrifying on one hand but somewhat beguiling on the other. It is overwhelming due its size, which required eight trailer loads to transport the materials for assembling.

Driving through Gallata Meadows, there are many sculptures to explore, such as the *Incredible Wind God Bird*, the extinct horse that may have appeared during the Pleistocene in Anza-Borrego and the tall and lanky giraffes that appear to be walking through a brushy African plain.

The Strange Elephant Trees

Elephant trees are said to be so rare that scientists denied there were any remaining. However, on any in a series of trails in an area along the eastern border of the Anza-Borrego State Park, these trees are there for all to see. They were not discovered until 1937. The shorter of the trails is called the Elephant Tree Discovery Trail, and as you scrutinize the lone tree on that trail, you will note that the wrinkled limbs are covered with peeling papery parchment-like bark resembling the surface of the folds of an elephant's hide. Although the trees are common in Baja California, they are considered an oddity in the California desert. They are not, however, deemed to be endangered.

Tapiadao Mud Caves and a Hollywood Surprise

The drive to Arroyo Tapiado in southern Anza-Borrego is full of surprises. The first sits in plain sight atop a sandstone hill—two street signs that read Hollywood Boulevard and Vine Street. A short climb takes hikers right to the signs to photograph and investigate and possibly find a pile of "stuff" that is called a geocache.

The caves are not visible from the road, but you might become suspicious when you see parked cars. Various cave explorers have mapped the caves and assigned names such as Chasm Cave, Plunge Pool Cave and E-Ticket

Among the many captivating attractions within the Anza-Borrego State Park are the Tapiado Mud Caves. Frequented by amateur spelunkers, winding below the earth, most caves change from enclosed caverns to slot canyons.

Cave. The spelunkers' number one rule is to carry three sources of light. Usually that would be a flashlight, a chemical tube light and perhaps an electric cave helmet. A hard hat might protect against a bruised forehead. Sturdy shoes and water are advisable. The caves wind through the earth, and there are few tight squeezes. Some of the caves change from enclosed caverns to slot canyons where you can look up and see the desert sky.

Purportedly five million years old, these sandstone tubes have been carved by water flowing through the dirt hills of Tapiado Canyon. You will see many bore holes throughout the area. With rain, these holes become larger, morph into caves and eventually become tunnels. Some caves boast large rooms, but there is little chance of getting lost because all paths either end abruptly or lead back into the main cave.

Spelunking in this area is great fun and a good activity for people of all ages.

WARNING: ABANDON YOUR TRIP AND RETURN TO SAFETY SHOULD IT RAIN! FLASH FLOODS HAVE CARVED THESE CAVES AND CAN DESTROY THEM.

The dirt roads to the cave area may be sandy and/or washboard. The ranger at the visitors' center can give up-to-date road conditions and detailed directions to the caves.

Anza-Borrego is different than most state parks in that you can camp anywhere. However, there are a number of campgrounds, and in the town of Borrego Springs there are hotels, private RV parks and campgrounds, shops and restaurants. It is truly a unique park, blessed with dark night skies ablaze with stars and an almost sure spectacular showing of wildflowers in the spring.

PEG LEG SMITH

Did you find a city of gold? There is a pile of rocks in the desert where you are invited to tell your story even if it were just in your imagination. But first, let's meet Peg Leg Smith.

Thomas Long "Peg Leg" Smith (1801–1866) was a fur trapper, trail guide and prospector, among less legal ventures. Born in Kentucky, he was known to have worked for such famed mountain men as Kit Carson and John Jacob Astor. When he joined an expedition headed west, he soon mastered several Native American languages.

One fateful day, Smith was shot in the knee by an Indian, after which he sported a wooden leg that he had whittled out of an oak stump. He thus

The story of Peg Leg Smith (1801–1886) is unbelievable, which is still the point today. His escapades are part of history and include the disputable fact that he lost a fortune in gold, the subject of constant searches. A plaque marks the spot where a nearby pile of rocks in the Anza-Borrego Desert invites fortune seekers to tell their fortune-hunting stories.

earned his nickname. Despite his disability, Peg Leg continued on and did well until the fur trade business hit hard times. He then employed his dark side and earned his living as a horse thief and worse. It is said that in the 1840s he organized the largest horse-stealing gang in the Southwest. But there were even darker stories about Peg Leg that describe his escapades involving the kidnapping and selling of Indian children.

All of this would have been lost to history but for an 1829 beaver trapping expedition that landed Peg Leg somewhere close to the Chocolate Mountains in the Colorado Desert near what is now called the Anza-Borrego Desert.

Lore has it that Peg Leg and his companion were trapped in a blinding sandstorm during which he discovered a pile of black rocks. He picked up a handful and stuffed them in his pocket and forgot about them for some time. Later, discovering the stones in his pocket, he investigated further and found that they contained pure gold encrusted with a black material. Now, exactly where did he find those stones he asked himself. He recalled climbing a small mountain in search of water, but blinded by sand, he became confused about the exact location.

Peg Leg's frustration has spread to those who dream of discovering a pile of gold. This was exacerbated by the fact that over the years he boasted to all who would listen about the discovery he found and lost. Peg Leg abandoned his search, moved north and lived the life of a bandit until he died in 1866 at the age of sixty-five. However, his story did not die with him. For years, the location of this lost pile of gold has been the subject of thousands of treks into the area by pick-and-shovel-toting treasure seekers. There are stories of successful searches where gold seekers claim to have discovered the source and made a fortune. There are stories of miners who have disappeared into the area never to return. And of course, there are the sad stories of those who ended up with squat.

Not everyone believes the story of this arguably dishonorable character, a legend that may have been lost but for a desert character and Hollywood set designer named Harry Oliver. Oliver published *The Desert Rat Scrap Book*, which was, as he explained, the world's smallest newspaper. Oliver was so fascinated with Peg Leg and his far-fetched stories that in 1916 he established a Peg Leg Club. In the late 1940s, the pile of rocks monument was thrown together in Anza-Borrego on Henderson Road. It appears as just that: a pile of rocks. It is often surrounded by campers taking advantage of the area's ordinance that allows camping outside of established campgrounds.

Since 1975, at this spot an annual Liar's Club contest is held on April 1, and here treasure seekers are invited to tell their stories. If a storyteller is convincing enough, then perhaps the audience will believe it. In the light of a roaring campfire, the participants who have been branded "pegophiles" recite pertinent lore as though it were accurately researched history. Their stories may be greeted with boos or approval but almost always with laughter and fun.

The monument sports a sign that reads, "Let those who seek Peg Leg's gold add ten rocks to this pile." A plaque at the site recites:

> PEG LEG SMITH. *Thomas L. Smith, better known as "Peg Leg Smith," 1801–1866, was a mountain man, prospector and spinner of tall tales.*

Legends regarding his lost mine have grown through the years. Countless people have searched the desert looking for its fabulous wealth. This gold mine possibly could be within a few miles of this monument. Registered Historical Landmark No. 750. Plaque placed by the California State Park Commission in cooperation with the Borrego Springs Chamber of Commerce, October 9, 1960.

The April 1 event requires sign ups at the site, and contestants are called on to perform in that order. Costumes are not required but are always met with great appreciation. Enthusiastic and embellished stories about searching for and perhaps finding the lost treasure are the usual theme.

To get to the Peg Leg Smith Liars' Contest, take Route S-22 east for about seven miles from Christmas Circle in downtown Borrego Springs. Travel past the airport, and follow the road around a hard left turn. Continue on S-22 until the road makes another hard turn, this time to the right. The road intersecting at the corner is Peg Leg Road. Turn left and find parking where you can. Bring blankets, lawn chairs and refreshments. The contest is during the evening and lasts between one and two hours.

Cowboy Man of Mecca

The Cowboy Man of Mecca near the Salton Sea must be lonely, having been placed far from most of his family. As he stands in a small strip mall parking lot, his fate is unknown, as is the case with everything near the Salton Sea, which ebbs and flows in the natural and political winds.

During the heyday of Route 66, a series of these fiberglass figures sprang up as roadside attractions. With growing traffic along the "mother road" from Santa Monica to Chicago, businesses were creative in luring travelers to their stores, restaurants or gas stations. The statues were there to lure business, and they were changed to meet the local theme. There is the Muffler Man, the Hot Dog Man and even the Green Astronaut Man in Wilmington, Illinois, which is also known as the Gemini Giant. The first of these oddities to appear was dubbed "Tall Paul" and popped up in the 1940s in the suburbs of Chicago.

Another favorite is arguably a younger version called the Chicken Boy. Standing proudly in Highland Park, California, the twenty-two-foot statue first appeared in Los Angeles atop a fried chicken restaurant between Fourth

The Cowboy Man of Mecca keeps a lonely vigil near the Salton Sea. Kin to the Muffler Man, the Hot Dog Man and even the Chicken Boy, the Cowboy has suffered many indignities. These fiberglass figures were made by International Fibreglass in Venice, California, and appear across the nation.

and Fifth Streets. When the restaurant owner died in 1984, the Chicken Boy was put into storage. At last, in about 2007, the fiberglass boy found a new home at 5558 Figueroa Avenue in Highland Park. Today, he towers above the buildings to the joy of passersby.

These iconic statues were born at the International Fiberglass Company in Venice, California, for use in outdoor advertising. Chicken Boy was altered from a Chicken Man that was originally created to be a Muffler Man or Paul Bunyan Man. His head was altered to resemble a chicken, and a bucket was fashioned to replace the hot dog or muffler.

These statues are familiar sights, especially along Route 66, but the bearded Cowboy Man near Mecca seems lost, and he has suffered much abuse. He was reportedly decapitated around 2001 and then went missing altogether. But he now stands proudly in front of the El Tompa Mini Mart, enjoying visitors who come to take his photo. His address is 93243 California 111, Mecca.

THE MOJAVE CROSS

Today, a seven-foot-high cross stands proudly atop a giant boulder called "Sunrise Rock" baked by the blazing Mojave Desert sun. It looks peaceful there, with little hint of the controversies, court cases, clashing of religious and nonreligious groups and negotiations surrounding its history. It is within the boundaries of the Mojave National Preserve.

The original cross was erected in 1934 by a prospector to commemorate soldiers killed in war. It was vandalized more than once, but a dedicated group of volunteers reconstructed it and charged themselves with its protection. However, the cross became the subject of a lawsuit, and lower court rulings declared it illegal because it existed on public land in violation of the United States Constitution's separation of church and state requirement.

After the finding of illegality by the lower court and the decision of the U.S. Supreme Court, an unlikely course of events occurred. A land swap was negotiated, and the land on which the cross stood was transferred to a veterans' group. It was therefore no longer on public land, and the violation was moot. This was validated by the ruling of the Supreme Court in 2010. Writing for the majority, Justice Anthony Kennedy wrote: "The goal of avoiding governmental endorsement [of religion] does not require eradication of all religious symbols in the public."

THE CROSS
Erected In Memory of
The Dead Of All Wars

Originally
Erected 1934 by Members
Veterans of Foreign Wars - Death Valley Post 2884

The Mojave Cross, erected in "memory of the dead of all wars," has fought a war itself to earn its resting place on Sunrise Rock within the Mojave National Preserve.

After the ruling, the cross suddenly disappeared and was later discovered in the Bay Area. It had reportedly been stolen by vandals, and when found, it had a note attached directing the finder to notify the authorities. It was then returned to Sunrise Rock and is protected by the Veterans of Foreign Wars.

The celebrated cross is located on an acre of land aside a two-lane asphalt road east of Cima Dome, about twelve miles south of I-5. It is surrounded by a cable barrier erected by the park service. Despite its primitive surroundings and tumultuous past, the cross is today the site of many rituals, including Easter sunrise services that are held annually by locals. A plaque on the boulder below the cross reads:

THE CROSS
Erected In Memory of
The Dead Of All Wars

PINNACLES OF TRONA

It would be difficult to hitch a ride on a spaceship to the moon, but arriving at the pinnacles of Searles Lake near Trona, California, you may experience the same feeling. It is an other-world-like scene, and the expectation of seeing someone from *Star Trek* is always there, perhaps because several episodes of the series were filmed at this spot.

Located in the California Desert National Conservation Area, there are more than five hundred tufa spires jutting from normally dry Lake Searles. These tufas are formed of calcium carbonate, and there are no two alike. There are tall, short, fat and skinny pinnacles, all surrounded by dried mud. It is not a good place to be in a rainstorm

The tufa formations grew 10,000 to 100,000 years ago when Searles Lake was part of an inland sea and the calcium-rich groundwater and alkaline lake water combined. These odd formations are among the most unique geological features in the California Desert Conservation Area. Over five hundred of these tufa spires rise from the lakebed, some up to 140 feet high. They create a strange city of high-rises. Taking advantage of the eerie scene, several movies have been filmed around the Pinnacles of Trona, including *Battlestar Galactica*, *Star Trek IV: The Final Frontier*, *Lost in Space* and *Planet of the Apes*.

The site is open year-round. The best times to visit are fall, winter and early spring. Good hiking and walking shoes are recommended. The dirt

The backdrop for many movies, including *Star Trek IV*, the Pinnacles of Trona has an "other-worldly appearance." The area is also the site of a unique desert event that attracts hundreds on an annual basis to nearby Trona's Gem-O-Rama.

access road is usually accessible by two-wheel drive vehicles. Following a rain, however, the road may be impassable to all vehicles, including four-wheel-drive vehicles.

Although the public is allowed to explore the Searles Lake area, it is designated as an Area of Critical Environmental Concern, so tread lightly.

The Searles Lake area, normally deserted but for an errant visitor, is a mob scene each October when the Searles Lake Gem and Mineral Society sponsors a Gem-O-Rama. This two-day event features a number of activities that culminate in a most unlikely exercise called the Blow Hole Field Trip. For a small fee, participants caravan behind a guide out a dirt road to an area at the lakebed. Here, crystals such as halite have formed in the brine water fifty feet below the surface. The Searles Lake Mineral Company drills several shafts fifty feet down to the brine water and, with help from navy explosive experts, places explosives down the shafts and then sets them off. This knocks crystals loose and propels them up the shaft.

All of this excitement is witnessed by those on the field trip. As a gasp emanates from the crowd, mud, water, rocks and crystals fly through the air and land on the surface of the lakebed. Of course, participants are held in a safe zone, but when the signal is given, it's a free-for-all. Bucket-toting men, women and children scramble to collect crystals. You keep what you get, and there is no limit. Collection usually entails some digging for the bigger rocks.

In the evening, the pastime is scrubbing dirt off the prized crystals. Those who don't know better soak them in water, only to wake up in the morning to find they have disappeared. They must be kept only in brine water to keep them from dissolving. As a fundraiser, local students sell containers of brine water.

Searles Lake is twenty miles east of Ridgecrest and ten miles from Trona, the gateway to Death Valley.

TEAKETTLE JUNCTION AND THE RACETRACK

There is an odd site in Death Valley on a road that ends at an even odder site.

Teakettle Junction is on the way to the famed rock-moving Racetrack. There is a sign announcing the junction on which hangs a variety of teakettles. Visitors are encouraged to paint or inscribe on a teakettle and

Teakettle Junction is a favorite stop for motorists headed to the Racetrack in Death Valley. No one is sure how this tradition began. It has been said it started when travelers wanted to mark a spot where water is found. However, no water has been found.

add it to the collection. No one knows why this nutty tradition began, though some believe it was to announce to desert wanderers that a water source was nearby. However, no one has found that water.

Rumor has it that locals, and no one is very local, clean off the teakettles once in a while and keep the area tidy.

Passing through will take you to the famed Racetrack, where tracks on the playa indicate that boulders large and small have traveled around on their own, leaving telltale tracks. However, in these days of surveillance cameras, the rocks can hardly expect to keep their secret.

At the Racetrack, you will find a parking area and a short path to the Grandstand, which is a large island of quartz manzonite. From there, you will have a grand view of the playa, which is about three miles long and two miles wide. It was formed at least ten thousand years ago when the area underwent climatic changes resulting in cycles of hot, cold and wet periods. The lake evaporated, leaving behind the beige mud you see today.

It is perhaps a combination of strong desert winds and slippery wet playa mud that is behind the mystery of moving rocks, but other theories catch the imagination—not the least of which is extraterrestrial.

SINGING EUREKA DUNES

To hike through a sand dune is to truly experience the desert. While many mountains of sand are found in the California deserts, the Eureka Dunes northwest of Death Valley are unique in many ways. Home to several protected plant species, the dunes exhibit another property that once experienced is hard to forget: they sing!

Covering an area of 3 square miles, these pale dunes rise 680 feet to the desert sky, making them one of the highest dune fields in North America. Despite their size, they may appear dwarfed with the Last Chance Mountains as a backdrop. Rising and falling like waves above the desert floor, the shadows and curves become mesmerizing, and to climb to the peaks is an intimate experience.

Stop and listen—do you hear a melody floating in the air? In the dry weather of the desert, the slipping of sand can produce unusual sounds, often described as booming, whistling, singing or barking. There are certain physical properties that must be present for these sounds to emit, such as the size of the grains of sand, the presence of silica and the humidity. At Eureka

Dunes, these properties are likely to be present. Because the movement of the sand is a catalyst for this natural sound phenomenon, it is more likely to occur as the sand avalanches under a hiker's footsteps.

The unique plants such as the Eureka Dune Grass, the Eureka Evening Primrose and the Shining Locoweed are not only fun to seek out, you can also thank them for the peacefulness experienced here. Because of their delicate existence, off-road vehicles and dune buggies are not allowed to enter the area, resulting in the quiet, contemplative aura of the dunes.

Eureka Dunes is one of the newest additions to Death Valley National Park due to an expansion in 1994. They are located in northern Inyo County and accessed by a gravel road that intersects with a paved road from Death Valley's Grapevine Canyon to Big Pine in the Owens Valley. Once at the dunes, there are no amenities save a lone restroom. Primitive camping is allowed at the northern end of the dune field. It is a quiet and desolate location that can soothe the soul. However, from time to time, the peacefulness is shattered by low-flying jets that race through the valley, adding to the peculiar scene.

PART II

Visiting History

WILLIE BOY'S GRAVE

Searching for Willie Boy's grave takes you to a wide expanse of a yucca-studded desert that, you may notice, resembles a scene from an old western movie. And indeed, it is the very site where the last western manhunt occurred in 1909, a historical event portrayed in the 1969 movie entitled *Tell Them Willie Boy is Here*, starring Robert Redford (the sheriff), Robert Blake (the elusive Chemehuevi-Paiute Indian called Willie Boy) and Katherine Ross (Carlotta, also called Lola, Willie Boy's doomed sixteen-year-old lover).

Massive chaotic boulders, intimate canyons and brushy yuccas provided ideal conditions for Willie Boy to hide with his arguably willing companion, Lola. The area is near the earthquake-famed town of Landers located on what is now BLM land, a haven for dirt bikers, ORVs and geocachers, some 125 miles east of Southern California's San Gabriel Valley.

Murdering Lola's father was twenty-eight-year-old Willie Boy's undoing, an act he claimed was in self-defense. Armed with a Winchester rifle, he escaped into the desert with Lola, who was later found dead, shot in the chest in Twentynine Palms. Whether her death was due to a deputy's errant shot, suicide or at the hands of her lover will never be known.

Pursued by a determined posse, all were amazed that Willie Boy survived in hiding for nearly three weeks. Eluding capture, he escaped into the Landers area, and as gunfire echoed off the canyon walls, a deputy was shot, compounding Willie Boy's problems and giving impetus to the posse's focus.

Willie Boy's grave marks a historical spot in the Landers area. It is there that the West's last manhunt ended and paved the way for a movie entitled *Tell Them Willie Boy Is Here*. To hike to the grave is to walk through history and relive this poignant event.

VISITING HISTORY

Back then, an Indian killing an Indian was one thing, but the shooting of the deputy bolstered the determination of the pursuers.

Willie Boy took cover on Ruby Mountain, keeping the posse and bounty hunters at bay for several days. In the end, the elusive Paiute was found dead from a gunshot wound, with some suspecting suicide and others claiming a posse victory. He was cremated and buried at the spot he was found.

The road to the gravesite is about two and a half miles long. Let your imagination loose, and you can almost smell the dust flying from galloping horses, hear the echo of bullets and feel the desperation of a cornered fugitive.

Approaching the grave marker, it appears somewhat irreverent, enclosed in barbed wire to discourage vandals. The marker merely reads: "Willie Boy, 1881–1909, The West's Last Famous Manhunt."

However, the site offers an opportunity to reflect on history and embrace an event that occurred in California's Wild West era.

According to a San Bernardino Sheriff's Association newsletter, the original historic landmark was erected by sheriff's rangers to mark where "Willie Boy, the mad dog of the Morongos, made his last defiant stand." After years of vandalism, it was replaced with the current bronzed plaque in 1987.

GPS coordinates: N 34 degrees 17.497, W 116 degrees 32.194.

Although the gravesite is officially the resting place of this young Paiute fugitive, there are those who believe that Willie Boy escaped. To hide their unsuccessful attempt to capture him, it is said the posse faked the cremation and burial so as to not admit their failure. Many believe Willie Boy lived out his life in the Indian world.

Another part of this story has also been lost. During the pursuit, the sheriff was called back to appear at the Mission Inn in Riverside as part of the greeting and security group for a visiting President Taft. When the sheriff's duties were over in that regard, he rejoined the posse and once again led the chase.

Willie Boy's Saloon and Dance Hall in Morongo is a museum-style eatery reflecting the gold rush era, including a nineteenth-century Brunswick bar and a deadwood jail cell that is rumored to have housed Wild Bill Hickok at one time.

The trail to Willie Boy's grave is along an old road that is now part of the Bighorn Wilderness. To get there, drive about six miles west on New Dixie Mine Road off CA 247 in Landers. There is a short spur to the right leading to some cables and a road closure.

Camping and hotels are nearby. This would be a good time to pay a visit to other unique California spots in that area. See: Giant Rock and Integratron.

WYATT EARP'S HOME, MINE

To see the pretty, modest blue cottage with a white picket fence in Vidal, California, one would never guess it was the home of the infamous tough gunslinger Wyatt Earp. He led a tumultuous life with a long line of legal and questionable occupations, but in the end, he and his wife, Josie, settled down in what was supposedly his only permanent residence. By that time, he had lived the lives of at least ten men and gained a reputation that lasted a lot longer than he did.

Wyatt Berry Stapp Earp lived in this cottage with his wife, Josephine Sarah Marcus Earp, from 1925 to 1928. From his home, he could work in his mine located nearby in the Whipple Mountains.

Born on March 19, 1848, Earp is probably the most well-known legend in the American West, and though he was a frontiersman, lawman and manual laborer, he was best known for his part in the 1881 gunfight near O.K. Corral, the greatest gunfight in the history of the West. Earp was uninjured in the

When the famed frontiersman-gunslinger-lawman Wyatt Earp finally settled down after a tumultuous life, he and his wife, Josephine Sarah Marcus Earp, seasonally lived in this modest cottage in Vidal.

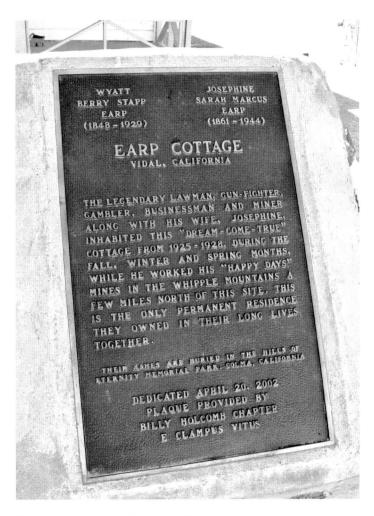

The modest cottage of Wyatt Berry Stapp Earp and Josephine Sarah Marcus Earp in Vidal is marked with a plaque dedicated on April 20, 2002, by the Billy Holcomb Chapter of E Clampus Vitus.

fight, and his brothers, Virgil and Morgan, lived despite their wounds. The gunslingers at the other end of Earp's weapon were killed.

Earp and Josephine lived in Alaska for a while but eventually returned to California and settled down in the little blue-trimmed cottage. There he wrote an accounting of his life, although it has been deemed mostly fiction. Ironically, he did become famous after he died, and the legend of Wyatt Earp is one of the most widely known stories in America, the subject of numerous books, movies and documentaries.

Wyatt Earp settled down to work his mining claims in the Whipple Mountains near his home in Vidal.

Wyatt Earp's Lucky Day mine sits crumbling in the desert today. A testimony to history, the claim was abandoned. A ray of sunlight passes through the mine ceiling, casting a light beam through the dusty darkness.

The Sonoran Desert town of Earp is located in Parker Valley near the California-Arizona border, close to Wyatt's cottage. It was originally named Dennan, founded in 1910, and changed to Earp in 1920. Tourists constantly snap photos of the post office and the fake small Earp grave site next to the structure. It is located on the south side of Highway 62 near the Parker Bridge.

Earp's mine is a bit difficult to find, but the entrance is passable for about fifty feet and then drops down a short way. There is no shoring, and trash is strewn around. About thirty feet into the darkness, a beam of light shines from a hole in the ceiling, casting a piercing ray to the mine floor. It is said that Earp discovered several deposits of gold and copper and filed more than one hundred mining claims. Before he had the cottage built, he and Josephine often camped at the mine during the mild times of the year. In the hot summer months, they were known to escape to Hollywood to rub elbows with the rich and famous.

Ironically, the little cottage was sold a few years back to Terry Ike Clanton, a direct descendent of the infamous Clantons who were Earp's rivals.

WHERE THE HELL IS CERRO GORDO?

Perched on a saddle atop a ridgeline of the Inyo Mountains, this historic silver-mining town offers an exciting adventure, though its thrill is rivaled by the road to reach it. It's on that road where you will see an odd site. Could it be a zip line? What are these buckets dangling vicariously from cables? The answer is a lesson in history and a tribute to man's ingenuity.

Starting at Keeler

Near the town of Lone Pine off Highway 395 at the foot of the Sierra Nevada Range, the road to Cerro Gordo starts across the highway from the living ghost town of Keeler that strides the east side of what was once Owens Lake. A stroll through Keeler yields a glimpse into the area's history. Pay no attention to the eyes peering through small cracks in the curtains of the area's homes. You may be surprised to find the Keeler post office open, though you may not see a living soul. Of note are remnants of the Keeler plunge, and the surfboard sign indicating Keeler "Beach."

The semi-ghost town of Keeler alongside the dry Owen's Lake may seem deserted, but parting curtains tell another story. The abandoned railway station is testament to the town's history.

Originally named "Hawley" and later named "Keeler," this is where a three-hundred-foot wharf was built for the steamship *Besse Brady* to carry seven hundred silver ingots at a time mined at nearby Cerro Gordo. This was when the lake actually had water in it. The legend goes that at least one ship sank, and the treasures it carried still lie below the lake bed. In 1883, after the *Besse* was destroyed by fire, a narrow-gauge railway transported the metals that were mined at Cerro Gordo.

The Curious Buckets

A trek through Keeler will put you in the mood to start the climb up the road to Cerro Gordo. The journey is almost as exciting as the destination. Under good conditions, the road can be negotiated without a four-wheel-drive automobile, but high clearance is advisable. There is a microwave station at the crest of the mountain for which the road is regularly maintained.

A few miles up the road, you will see an odd sight. It is here that a tram house once stood before it was removed in 1959. However, steel cables and a

The journey to "Fat Hill" is almost as exciting as the actual town. Once in town, visitors may be treated to a casual tour by the caretaker that may include the mill, store, museum, hotel, the bunkhouse and desert art.

few of the ore buckets that at one time transported silver, lead and zinc down the mountain can be easily seen. This is quite a sight and tells the story of how mining was once accomplished. There are rumors that mineworkers up the mountain would jump on the ore cars for a ride down the hill and later bring groceries up via the buckets.

Continuing up the road, you will find precipitous drops, but the road is wide, which may dispel any fears. As you climb, you may find yourself gazing at the Sierra Nevadas across the Owens Valley and eventually will reach a point where you feel equal to the height of that range. Long before reaching Cerro Gordo, your presence will be known, and normally the caretaker will greet you and offer a tour. There is a nominal fee over which a tip is usually called for.

Discovered by Mexican prospectors in 1865, Cerro Gordo was a treasure trove. Large amounts of silver were extracted from the many mines in the area. When word got out about the rich "Fat Hill," the Union Mining Company was formed and the town began to grow. Two large smelters were constructed. The two-story Great American Hotel was built and became the focal point of the town, which, at its peak, was home to more than three thousand people.

But as is the usual story, this booming town died when mining proved to not be cost effective, and deserted of its population, it became a true ghost town, some say second only to nearby Bodie.

A city girl named Jody Stewart on a whim visited her uncle, who had become the owner of Cerro Gordo, and she immediately felt connected to this rusty old town. She made a life-changing decision and, with her boyfriend, later her husband, Mike Peterson, moved into the town and gave it her feminine touch. Today, you can see the result of her work when you tour the hotel and enjoy its furnishings and atmosphere. She dressed up the rooms in the tin boardinghouse in Victorian style and even made the detached outhouse feel like a fancy loo. At one time, groups could rent out the rooms and bed down for the weekend in the town.

Sadly, Jody died, and not long after, Mike passed away. The spirit of the town waned. Jody is buried on a high point of the hill.

Visiting the town is a hit-or-miss project and depends on whether the caretaker is there and the condition of the road. But even the walk through Keeler and the short drive to the ore buckets and cable will make the journey worthwhile. And then, of course, you will find yourself on the beautiful scenic Highway 395, which boasts many rewards of its own.

To reach the road to Cerro Gordo from the south, exit Highway 395 by turning right on CA 190 East (go 14.6 miles), then left on CA 136 West (go

Visitors to the old California Hotel in Cerro Gordo have a difficult time resisting the urge to belly up at the bar or play a round of poker in the poker room. Here, Joe McVey plays the part.

4.6 miles) and then right on Cerro Gordo Road, where you will start to climb the hill. To trek through Keeler, pass Cerro Gordo Road, and in a short distance, Keeler is on your left. Then backtrack to Cerro Gordo Road and start your adventure up the mountain to the ore buckets.

RANDSBURG

Once a gold-mining destination, Randsburg is now a place for city dwellers to visit if they are looking for a historic mining town. Located in the northern Mojave Desert, it is not a ghost town, and many storefronts on the main street

Above: With antique and "junk" stores galore, wandering down the main street of Randsburg can take a while. Favorites are Charlie's Oar House Antique Store, the town museum, the general store and the White House Saloon. Most of the buildings are original.

Left: The 1897 Santa Barbara Church in Randsburg burned down soon after it was constructed. It was rebuilt in 1904. It is probably the most photographed structure in the old mining town.

are open to the public. It is a tourist-friendly town but thankfully lacks staged shootouts. However, there is the town's big event held the first weekend of September every year featuring animals, cowboys, live music and food.

One favorite draw is the 1904 soda fountain and the "Black Bart" banana split dessert offered at the general store. Belly up to the counter with a view of the working old malt machines or choose to sit at the tables where you are likely to be joined by hordes of dirt bikers of all ages. Across Butte Avenue is the White House Saloon, still a favorite stopover for a drink, a meal and people watching. There are gift shops, many run by bearded desert dwellers; a mining museum; and, the oddity of the area, the old jail, which offers a coveted photo op.

The mines of the area have produced over one million ounces of gold. Today, the gold-mining activities have been replaced by tourist shops selling antiques. Part-time prospectors and off-roaders stop in town for food and a rest. Visitor friendly, there is a local park in the heart of town with picnic tables and restrooms.

Gold was discovered at Rand Mine near the site in 1895, and a mining camp quickly formed. The camp was named Rand Camp, and both the mine and the camp were named after a gold-mining region in South Africa. The first post office at Randsburg opened in 1896.

A plaque at the town jail erected by E Clampus Vitus reads:

> RANDSBURG, CALIFORNIA. *Gold was discovered on the slope of Rand Mountain in 1895. From this discovery the Town of Randsburg sprang up almost overnight. By 1899 the town had over 3500 residents. Randsburg boasted a 300-stamp mill and conservative estimates are that $30,000 in gold was taken out of the mines in the area during the town's boom years. From 1875 until about 1933 the Yellow Aster Mine produced almost $375,000,000 worth of gold at the old gold prices of about $20.00 per ounce. The bar and the White House Saloon were host to many a miner, cowboy, farmer, Indian and Clamper during the peak of the mining district. Plaque dedicated on October 8, 1989, by John P. Squibob, Peter Lebeck, Slim Princess and Billy Holcomb Chapters of the Ancient and Honorable Order of E Clampus Vitus.*

Randsburg is located on the west side of I-395 between Kramer Junction to the south and Ridgecrest to the north.

Indian Wells Brewing Company

Dubbed "the biggest little brewery in the world," this unique stop is a favorite for visitors headed to Randsburg from the south by way of I-14. It is located on a historic artesian spring. This microbrewery, which offers a tasting room, boasts twenty kinds of beer and a number of soft drinks with unusual labels such as "Martian Poop Soda."

It is said that a group of fortune hunters heading for the Sacramento gold fields in 1849 took a shortcut branching off from the Santa Fe Trail, got lost and ended up on the spot where the brewery is located. Here they found the pure water that saved them.

The brewery is located at 2565 State Highway 14, Inyokern, California, 93527.

ZZYZX

To find this place in the phone book, you will have to go to the very end. And that is on purpose because the person who named it wanted to have the last word.

There are so many quirky facts about this place that it's hard to know where to start. It is located off I-15 near the town of Baker and sits on the shore of the waterless Soda Lake. A four-and-a-half-mile partially paved road from the highway leads to the compound.

Zzyzx today is the California State University Desert Studies Center, but in the past, it was known as the Zzyzx Mineral Springs and Health Spa. Rich folks and movie stars were regular visitors until it came to its eventual demise.

Man has always been attracted to this area because of its treasure: water. For centuries, man trekked through this part of the Mojave Desert, first Mohave and Chemehuevi Indians and later Spanish explorers, all rewarded by drinkable spring waters. In the 1860s, it became a U.S. Army outpost

Opposite, top: Today Zzyzx serves as the California State University Desert Studies Center. In an earlier life, it was known as Zzyzx Mineral Springs and Health Spa. Born from a mining claim, the story of this oddly named site includes homeless people from Los Angeles, stars from Hollywood and a charismatic man who, in the end, could not hold it together.

Remnants of Carl Springer's signature mud baths remain on the property, although not operable. He made money from his health, promoting pills and lotions, most of which contained crystals from the nearby waterless Soda Lake.

called Camp Soda Springs. Miners descended on the area in an attempt to extract minerals from the lakebed, and the Tonopah and Tidewater Railroad eventually chugged by. Prospectors and treasure seekers frequented the water-bearing area.

The odd turn of events took place in 1944 with the arrival of Curtis Howe Springer, a radio evangelist and self-proclaimed minister who found the area to be a perfect place for his dream of building a health resort. Springer filed a mining claim and soon employed homeless men who had been living in a mission he ran in Los Angeles. Construction on the site and decades of questionable ventures began.

This was not Springer's first attempt. He had tried to establish health spas before in several areas of the country, but none had been successful because he lacked the cash to continue. However, Zzyzx proved to be a winning proposition for several decades.

The land he claimed was falling apart. Remnants of the old fort were strewn about, and what was left of the old railroad station had all but disappeared. The men he employed were housed in tents and began building the concrete structures that would soon house hundreds of clients.

Springer called himself "Doc," and while concocting lotions, creams and vitamins, he turned the dreary mining claim into a modern health spa. The clear clean crystal spring waters were enough to build a clientele, but promises of sustained youthfulness and health didn't hurt. Springer built a sixty-room hotel, a two-story castle, a church and even an airport called the Zyport. He built rooms along a small lake in the compound. He also built a dining hall, library and lecture room and a pool house. Many of these buildings continue to be utilized today. Springer named the main road through the compound "Boulevard of Dreams."

There were no set fees for those who came, but many made large enough donations to keep the enterprise afloat.

Although history points to Springer as a scam artist, outlaw, cheater and such, he was responsible for turning the dilapidated hellhole into a modern spa and, in the mix, gave hope and jobs to the many Los Angeles homeless he employed. He gave no thought to lying about his credentials, presenting himself as a doctor, claiming all sorts of bogus educational degrees and selling worthless concoctions claiming outrageous cures.

As word spread of the magic of Springer's products and spa waters, the area took on a mystical aura that was promoted further by his trips to Los Angeles on the lecture circuit. He was reportedly a man of charisma and was touted as a masterful lecturer. Many felt they knew him because for decades he had a syndicated evangelical radio program that was broadcasted throughout the country. He was a likeable man, one whom people immediately trusted. He was a big man and sported a full head of red hair and a demeanor that was alluring.

Springer's health food products—advertised as cures for a number of maladies, including indigestion, fatigue and even baldness—were ordered from all over the country. Some products were touted to prolong life. Most products were created from crystals mined from Soda Lake.

Along with his wife, Springer enjoyed hundreds of loyal patrons, many of whom returned time and again to enjoy the desert sun, soak in the spas and partake of the health food. There were parties, entertainment, religion and relaxation all orchestrated by the "doc" himself.

While many considered him the king of healthy living, the American Medical Association called him the king of quacks. Springer's dream began to crumble when the government ceased turning a blind eye to his little kingdom and all hell broke loose. The Pure Food and Drug Administration accused him of false advertising, the IRS hit him for tax evasion and the Bureau of Land Management took over his land when it was discovered that he did not have a legal right to it.

Once on top of the world, Springer was suddenly the focus of a government investigation that began perhaps when he advertised a bold move to sell plots of land on "his property" for customers to purchase and build their own homes. His successful endeavor in jeopardy, he was publically branded a scammer and an outlaw. The government claimed he was illegally squatting on public land, a charge on which he was tried in the courts and found guilty. He was imprisoned for a short time and later wrote a book about the court proceedings that stripped him of his land. He entitled the book *The Legal Rape of Zzyzx*.

Doc Springer left Zyzzx in 1974, and although it is said that he never returned, that isn't exactly true. In 1976, a group from the California universities that had been given authorization by the Bureau of Land Management to utilize the area as a Desert Studies Consortium was surprised when Springer showed up and asked them to gather 'round. He purportedly told them he was innocent of the charges and that the land was his. He insisted he had no problem with the land being used for a desert studies center and that such was his idea way in the beginning. However, he said he still felt he was the rightful owner, adding, "This land belongs to God and should be used for the greater good."

Springer and his wife moved to Las Vegas. He died in 1985 at the age of eighty-nine.

The complex has been renovated in part by the Desert Studies Center and is used for classes featuring such subjects as birding, photography, geology and astronomy. The pond-like lake is full and surrounded by palms and unique plants. It is also a likely spot to focus binoculars on a green heron or perhaps a Lucy's warbler. Springer's original cross-shaped pool and adjacent mud baths are now dry but still there to see. It is a perfect spot for desert studies due to its diverse geological, biological and cultural resources.

Storage areas in the rear of the compound house quirky signs and memorabilia from days gone by.

There is not an open invitation for guests to poke around the compound, but tourists who are respectful to the classes in session are allowed to explore the grounds during the daylight hours. Exit I-15 at Zzyzx Road and turn left.

GOFFS

An Oddity of Oddities

Sadly, the community of Goffs in San Bernardino County is an oddity in itself. There are few places that have successfully managed to covet the past and rescue historical artifacts from certain disappearance. In Goffs, under the guidance of Dennis Casebier, thousands of oral histories of families who populated this area of the Mojave Desert have been recorded. The compound, the artifacts and the oral histories are now under the care of the Mojave Desert Heritage and Cultural Association.

The town was created in 1883 on what was to become the main line of the Santa Fe Railroad. As the years brought more and more train traffic, Goffs became a main entry point into the East Mojave and continues that role today.

The town began to swell with railway employees and their families, and as the population demanded, a schoolhouse was called for. One was built in 1914 and featured a unique mission-style design.

As the town continued to grow, a former wagon road that ran along the railroad tracks became the National Old Trails Road and eventually became a segment of the famed Route 66. When Route 66 became realigned, it took second to the new road that opened in 1931. Although its population blossomed when more than ten thousand World War II U.S. Army troops were stationed there, it was a brief event. At their

From the air, the Old Route 66 compound in Goffs looks sparse, but it is home to the largest collection in existence of oral histories of Mojave Desert families who lived in the area. It is now home to the Mojave Desert Heritage and Cultural Association and is an outdoor museum.

departure, the town was privately owned for years and fell into disrepair when the owners moved out.

Enter Dennis Casebier, and in time, he and his wife, Jo Ann, came to the rescue. They moved into the town and since that time have changed the compound into an indoor/outdoor museum with a collection of thousands of history-related documents and books on the area, including the oral histories that fill the six-thousand-square-foot library now housed in a replica of the old Goffs Railway Depot (1902–56). There is also a working ten-stamp mill, a courthouse, a bunkhouse, an Atlantic-Pacific boxcar and hundreds of additional mining items.

The Casebiers and their dedicated, hardworking crew of volunteers renovated the schoolhouse, which today serves as a museum. Many of the oddities in Goffs may be found on the Outdoor Museum Nature Trail and elsewhere on the grounds. The Miner's Cannon, which purportedly was found deep in the tunnels of an East Mojave mine, is on display and occasionally is the source of an earthshaking boom that reverberates throughout the area. Another oddity is the Fraser-Chalmers ten-stamp mill

The 1914 schoolhouse in Goffs was nearly lost to vandals and the elements when it was rescued by author-historian Dennis Casebier and a host of volunteers. Today, its unique Mission-style design shines, and the interior serves as a museum.

A replica of the Goffs Railway Depot (1902–56) serves as a repository for the Mojave Desert archives. Thousands of oral histories and vintage photos are stored there.

The so-called Miner's Cannon, presumably rescued from the remnants of an East Mojave mine, occasionally emits an earthshaking boom that reverberates through the area.

that was constructed in 1890. With determination, skill and research on behalf of the volunteers, the mill is now in working order.

Hundreds of interesting historical items are on display, clearly marked and described in a brochure that sets forth the locations and history of each. The center is open to the public free of charge as follows: October 1–June 30: Saturday, Sunday and Monday 9:00 a.m. to 4:00 p.m. For other days and times, call (760) 733-4482 for a reservation, or e-mail info@mdhca.org.

Goffs is located on the National Old Trails Road, the original alignment of U.S. Highway 66, along the Burlington Northern Santa Fe Railway. It is about one hundred miles from Las Vegas, Barstow and Twentynine Palms.

HISTORIC KEYS RANCH

Walking through the Keys Ranch in Joshua Tree National Park is to go back in time and visualize what life was like for the brave souls who settled in the desert and persevered. The ranch has been preserved, and tours are led by the park service.

Bill Keys lived a rather tumultuous life before settling down on the ranch. He left home at the age of fifteen and joined Teddy Roosevelt's Rough Riders. However, before his group left for Cuba, he broke his foot and was left behind. He worked for a while as a ranch hand and smelter operator and even became a deputy sheriff in Mohave County, Arizona. After heading to Death Valley in 1906, Keys purportedly began a friendship with Death Valley Scotty, a relationship that ended in a famous swindle known as the Battle of Wingate Pass.

Keys's friendship with Scotty was almost his undoing. He should have known better than to get mixed up in Scotty's shenanigans. As usual, Scotty was shooting off his mouth to some rich easterners, and they began to take an interest in what Scotty described as a very lucrative mining operation. They almost had to beg Scotty to let them grubstake his claim. After months of reporting back to them about the success of the mine, but without sending any money, these gentlemen began to get suspicious and announced plans to come to California and see the mine for themselves.

What was Scotty to do? There was no mine, no success and no money. So Scotty dreamed up a plan and talked Keys and a man named Bob Belt into helping him out. When the investors arrived, Scotty set out to lead them to the mine. As planned, they were ambushed by robbers—an event he explained was not out of the ordinary in those parts. But then the plan turned sour. Keys and Belt were supposed to shoot Scotty's burro, but the errant bullet hit Scotty's brother instead. Furious with the turn of events, Scotty yelled up to his cohorts bawling them out for shooting his brother instead of his burro. Hearing this, the easterners knew they had been swindled and swore to get even. They did.

Unfortunately for Scotty, the lawsuit went before a judge who had always been suspicious about his business dealings and did not believe there ever was a real mine. After an investigation, Scotty was arrested. Keys and Belt had returned to the desert but were brought back to San Francisco for the superior court hearing. They were charged with assault with a deadly weapon. After a jurisdictional issue arose, the hearing moved to Independence, but the witnesses involved did not want to spend time in Independence so they left and the case ended.

Keys fled to the Twentynine Palms area, where he became friends with a cattle rustler named Jim McHaney. McHaney was the owner of a ranch but was unable to keep up with the maintenance of his property due to failing health. Keys helped him out, and eventually, when his friend died, he took over the ranch and the nearby Desert Queen Mine.

In 1918, Keys married Francis M. Lawton and they raised their children on the ranch. The family raised chickens, turkeys and cows. Their garden was well tended and fruitful. However, Keys was once again in trouble in a dispute over the Wall Street Mill. He shot and killed Worth Bagley, was convicted of murder and spent time in the San Quentin Prison. His prison time offered the opportunity for Keys to do something he had no time to pursue before: get an education. He was paroled in 1950 and pardoned in 1956, largely through the efforts of Erle Stanley Gardiner, American lawyer and author, probably best known for his Perry Mason detective series.

Bagley is buried near the Keys property and his headstone reads:

> *Here is where Worth Bagley bit the dust at the hand of W.F. Keys.*
> *May 11, 1943.*

The ranch is a National Historic Site within the Joshua Tree National Park. The ranger-led tour includes the ranch house, the schoolhouse that Keys had built for his children, a store and a workshop. The orchard has been replanted. Strewn about are farm equipment, old rusted cars and mining tools that tell the story of the hard life the Keyses endured.

Tours are held regularly on a reservation basis and there is a fee. Tickets may be purchased at the Joshua Tree and Oasis Visitors Centers and the ranger will provide a map with directions to the remote canyon in which the ranch is located.

Kelso Station and Dunes

The story of the Kelso Station is one of the few examples in which an almost vanished historical site was about to disappear completely but was saved by an occurrence that no one could have predicted years ago. Thankfully, today the station is an experience available to all who seek an adventure in the California desert.

The first depot owned by the Los Angeles and Salt Lake Railroad, Kelso opened in 1905 and later added the Kelso Clubhouse and Restaurant, which came to be known as the Beanery, to serve the employees and passengers on passing trains. It was also a necessary water stop for the steam engine trains.

The 1905 Kelso depot was so close to death that its friends and supporters had almost given up hope. The unlikely savior was the Desert Protection Act of 1994, resulting in the East Mojave National Scenic Area, which became the Mojave National Preserve. Now under the care of the National Park Service, the depot has been renovated. It is a wonderful sight to behold.

Kelso station is an example of the surviving mid-1920s-era Mission Revival and Spanish Colonial Revival architecture. The grounds were maintained, and the station was surrounded by green gardens. It was perhaps presented as a showcase among stations in order to compete with the Santa Fe depots that boasted the Harvey House restaurants.

Once booming, the depot saw a sharp decline in train traffic at the end of World War II and a further reduction when the Vulcan Mine closed in 1947. The slow period was ended with a rise in activity during the Korean War, but unable to compete with the high-powered diesel-electric locomotives, the station closed to passenger train traffic in 1964. The lunchroom, however, remained open for a while.

Desert travelers over the next several decades watched the decline of the once showcased station. The paint peeled. The gardens wilted. The roof caved. Graffiti marked the walls. A group bent on saving the station created a Save Kelso Fund, but the necessary funds were not raised. The Bureau of Land Management took responsibility for the station, but it seemed only a matter of time before the station remains were hauled off.

As fate would have it, the savior of the building was the passage of the California Desert Protection Act of 1994, which resulted in the East Mojave National Scenic Area becoming the Mojave National Preserve, and the Kelso Depot became the responsibility of the National Park Service. Renovation of the station began in 2002, and in 2006, it became the headquarters for the preserve. Gardens were planted, the roof restored, walls painted and the interior restored to its former glory. Dormitory rooms were renovated, as were the baggage room and ticket office to the delight of tourists anxious to see what it was like in the "olden days." Downstairs housed a new café with a lunch counter, and several rooms contain exhibits with artifacts and photos of Kelso's past. There are outside picnic tables and restrooms. An informational film is also shown. It is open from 9:00 a.m. to 5:00 p.m. daily, only closed on Christmas Day. On the opening day of the renewed station, Huell Howser was present and produced a show, interviewing old-timers who frequented the area when it was in its heyday.

From I-15, exit at Kelbaker Road and continue southeast to Kelso. From I-40, exit at Kelbaker Road and continue north to Kelso.

Near the station, a trek up the majestic Kelso Dunes is not an easy task. For each step you take, you may slip back a bit, but upon reaching the peak, the view is spectacular. These dunes are known to emit a "boom" or a "rumbling" sound when the rounded rose quartz sand grains slide over the underlying surface.

The tallest of the dunes rises 650 feet above the desert floor, and the dune field covers forty-five square acres of desert. Climbing the soft sand can be a mystical and contemplative experience since off-road vehicles are not allowed. The dunes lie just southwest of the Kelso Depot.

Charm of Nipton

This charming Mojave Desert town is the gateway to the Mojave National Preserve and offers a glimpse of what inns and trading posts were like during California's mining and ranching days.

Visitors from all over the world stop in to relax and enjoy the view of the vast desert that surrounds the outpost. There is almost always someone stationed at the railroad tracks to photograph an oncoming train, and everyone gives the obligatory wave to the engineer. Lunch at the Whistle Stop Café is a must. The trading post is known for its hospitality, supply of books and maps, Native American jewelry and crafts and, especially, its history in selling winning lottery tickets.

Near the café and trading post is the Hotel Nipton, which was originally constructed between 1904 and 1910. The Spanish Territorial–style building was restored in 1986 and refurbished in 2004. It is open as a bed-and-breakfast, and the five small rooms surround a reading and sitting room where coffee and snacks magically appear. It would be difficult to resist lounging on the front porch that overlooks a rock garden with a maze of trails, native plants and a superb view of the wide expanse of desert. Nearby are picnic tables, a reflection pond and an eco-lodge with tented cabins that are based on a design by Frank Lloyd Wright.

It wasn't that long ago when Nipton had deteriorated to the point of earning the label of ghost town. In 1984, the outpost was purchased by Gerald Freeman, who became enthralled with the place while he was prospecting in the area. The Cal Tech–trained geologist reportedly purchased the town for $200,000 and made it his mission to bring it back to life.

Nipton is certainly a town that went from rags to riches. Well, maybe not riches, but it has earned its place as a historical town of charm and hospitality. The parking lot is almost always busy with rental RVs driven by travelers from all over the world and such an odd human assortment as roving motorcycle caravans, robed monks and motorists who spy the outpost and cannot resist a look-see.

Nipton is located two miles from the Nevada-California border in east San Bernardino County, ten miles off I-15.

MITCHELL CAVERNS

This geologic wonderland has had a rough life, and its woes continue today. It is included in this book because it is certainly an adventure worth pursuing, but at the moment, the actual caverns are closed due to financial reasons on behalf of the California State Park Service. Although the caverns are under the jurisdiction of the state park system, geographically they are surrounded by the National Mojave Preserve. At this time, renovations to the park facilities and visitors' center are underway, and as grant monies and donations are received, the park service together with the Save Mitchell Caverns organization hope the caverns and visitors' center will soon be open to the public once again. They owe it to the Mitchell family.

Located near the Route 66 desert town of Essex, the caverns have attracted thousands of motorists enjoying an opportunity to jump off the mother road for a respite in their travels.

There was once a place the Chemehuevi called "the eyes of the mountain," which is what we know today as Mitchell Caverns. The caves, located in the Providence Mountains of California's Mojave Desert, became the property of Jack and Ida Mitchell through a series of mining ventures. They remained in their care from 1934 to 1954. The couple recognized the tourist potential in this naturally decorated limestone cavern. However, Route 66 was some twenty-two miles from the caves, and a decent road up the mountain was a must.

A determined man, Jack knew what he must do. The primitive prospector's trail leading from the Route 66 town of Essex to the cave must be forged into a road good enough for "city folk who had money to spend." Jack became a trailblazer, chopping at plants with a hatchet under the burning desert sun. One day while in town, he met a trucker who was hauling a caterpillar tractor. Now Jack was a convincing man, and soon the caterpillar was at work blazing a road up the mountain.

This was but one of Jack's projects. Tourists would need food, water and maybe a night's stay in addition to a cave tour. A creative couple, the Mitchells made furniture from old auto cushions, Choy cactus and the skeleton heads of sheep. He also appointed himself "a one-man chamber of commerce," advertising his "resort" to attract customers. He had to spread the word that "Essex was a town, not an automobile."

From their front porch, the Mitchells enjoyed an unobstructed view across the subtle hues of the vast desert. They would constantly spot dust clouds rising into the desert air as visitors drove up the dirt road to visit. Cave tours included the opportunity to behold ornate speleothems and to learn about the paleontological and archaeological finds in the area. As word spread, Jack and Ida found their abode to be a popular destination for tourists motoring along Route 66.

Jack reportedly escorted more than forty thousand tourists through the caverns over a period of twenty years. Sadly, in 1954, at the age of seventy-two, he died in an unfortunate accident. Coincidentally, before his death in order to preserve the caves and the homestead, he had made arrangements for the state park to take over the caverns.

Crafting furniture from Choy cactus and skeleton heads of sheep, the home of Jack and Ida Mitchell became a "resort" where they entertained customers who stayed the night after touring the limestone caverns.

The area became a state recreation area in 1956 and now sits in the midst of the Mojave National Preserve. A visitors' center and exhibits are located in what had served as the Mitchell home from which a half mile, mostly level trail, leads to the cave entrance. When open, the state rangers lead groups through about a quarter mile of the cave and narrate the geological and historical significance of the unique limestone caverns.

The caverns are located off I-40 East from Barstow; exit at Essex and follow the signs.

BALLARAT

It was a rowdy town as witnessed by a population of about 450 people and seven saloons. Ballarat followed the rise and fall of most towns of the time as it began to grow in 1896 to supply goods for the mines nearby. Anchored by a nearby reliable water source, the population grew despite the desolate Mojave Desert location near the Panamint Mountains and Death Valley. Many of Ballarat's structures were constructed with mud.

Why Ballarat? It was named after an Australian gold-mining camp that was the first in that country to discover gold, and it was there that the world's largest nugget was found—143 pounds! The name was at the insistence of an Australian immigrant named George Riggins.

Missing in California's Ballarat was a church, but it did boast a Wells Fargo station, three hotels, a post office, a school and a jail. After working hard in the mines, Ballarat men returned home to relax and patronize the saloons.

As nearby mines began to decline, and with the closing of the Radcliffe Mine in 1903, the town buckled, and many residents moved on to more lucrative communities. One resident who decided to stay after the town died was Seldom Seen Slim, who continued on until he died in 1968 at the age of eighty-six. He was buried in Ballarat's Boot Hill, and his epitaph exhibits the words he was known for: "Me lonely? Hell no! I'm half coyote and half wild burro." His grave site headstone remains to the delight of tourists snapping photos.

For years, the withering town survived with a few full-time residents, and then along came a man with a dream. He was Neil Cummings, who purchased acreage just east of town with the aim of developing it into a tourist destination to take advantage of the warm desert weather. He made some improvements such as an RV park and a store, but his endeavor failed and he abandoned the area in 1988. Scenes in the movie *Easy Rider* were filmed there.

Still, Ballarat hung on with a few residents, and such is the state of the town today. Although some still call it home, most of the town has crumbled. Often people may be seen strolling among collapsed and melting adobe structures, but most are tourists with curious eyes on this historic town. Among the remnants strewn around is a green 1942 Dodge power wagon that was purportedly driven by a Charles Manson gang member named Tex Watson when the group fled Barker Ranch. The entire area is certainly a photographer's paradise and a place to contemplate the ironies of life.

Tourists are thrilled when they find the remaining store and museum open, and they may even run into the town's "caretaker," Rock Novak, who took over the responsibility when his father, George, died in 2011 at the age of ninety.

Just outside of town is the Pleasant Canyon Loop Trail, which winds through several of the mines and mining camps that once supported the town. This is a scenic high-elevation four-by-four trail that is susceptible to water erosion and landslides. There is a lot to see and explore along the trail. Much of the area is owned by the Briggs Corporation, and it graciously allows the public to use the cabins on its property free of charge.

PIONEERTOWN

Not exactly a town but definitely not a ghost town, Pioneertown near the community of Yucca Valley is an odd place that is certainly worth a visit. After a walk through the dusty "Mane" Street and a drink at Pappy & Harriet's Pioneertown Palace, visitors appreciate how unusual this little unincorporated community is.

Built in 1946 as a "façade" for the filming of westerns, it went a little further. Instead of the usual façades, the buildings along the street are real buildings in which people live. During movie shoots, the buildings were occupied by actors and crew on location.

Roy Rogers was among the original investors in the town, which has served as the scene of more than fifty films plus several television shows during the

The Pioneertown Bowl was known as the oldest bowling alley in continuous use in the United States when it ceased business several years ago. Film crews passed their off-stage time in movie-scene Pioneertown.

It is said that Roy Rogers tossed out the first ball at the Pioneertown bowling alley in 1949. Nearby students reset the pins until automated pin-setting equipment was installed in the 1950s. In better days, when open, the public could enjoy a game at this iconic bowling alley.

1940s and '50s. Some of the most popular movies filmed in Pioneertown include *Judge Roy Bean*, *The Oregon Trail* and *Winning of the West*. In addition, it served as a favorite location spot for many of the episodes of the Gene Autry series during the 1950s.

A favorite structure in the past that remains today is the wooden six-lane Pioneer Bowl bowling alley at which, it is said, Roy Rogers rolled out the first ball in 1949. Students from a nearby high school were employed to replace the bowling pins until automated pin-setting equipment was installed in the 1950s. An old-fashioned soda fountain adds to the scene. It was known as the oldest bowling alley in continuous use in the United States until it closed several years ago. A peek through the window is still possible.

Sun-bleached desert glass, rusted toys and appliances decorate the yards. One yard exhibits nearly a dozen manual typewriters lined up in a row as though a secretarial crew will show up at any minute. Other yards are decorated with desert "junk" or "treasures"—whichever people choose to call it. Roosters crow, dogs bark and tourists wander through town taking photos.

After a stroll through this unusual town, a meal and drink at Pappy & Harriet's Pioneertown Palace is called for. When the movie-filming days ended, the building was privately purchased and opened as a cantina—"an outlaw biker burrito bar." It remained a rowdy, fun-filled bar until it closed. The establishment was later purchased by Harriet Aleba and her husband, Claude "Pappy" Allen, who renamed the place Pappy & Harriet's Pioneertown Palace.

Today, Pappy & Harriet's is the "in place" to frequent. After driving on a small, dark and barely inhabited road for four miles off Highway 62 in Yucca Valley, you arrive at Pappy & Harriet's. Despite the vast dirt parking lot, it is difficult to find a parking spot for the voluminous amount of cars and motorcycles. Once inside, the music blasts, the bar is hopping, cue balls click, beer flows and the dance floor is home to the two-step. It is a gathering place for cowboys and girls, bikers, senior citizens, children and usually a host of desert rats. The live music features bands from all over the country, and on the "off night," it is open mic, when local talent pleases the crowd.

This establishment has earned the reputation as one of the Top Ten Gems in the country. There is a cover charge for some of the more well-known performers, but usually the music is free. The menu is varied, ranging from burgers to rib eyes. The waitresses keep a friendly demeanor in the midst of the chaos. There is also a patio seating area around the ever-sizzling barbecue.

Too tired to drive home? Just walk out the back door and arrive at the Pioneertown Motel. This rustic eighteen-room lodge also features seventeen corrals for use by horse people. The guest rooms are constructed from railroad ties.

Pioneertown is truly a remarkable place, balanced between the past and present. It was nearly destroyed in the July 11, 2006 Sawtooth Complex fire that destroyed much of the landscape and some nearby houses.

Pioneertown is located on Pioneertown Road off Route I-62 in the town of Yucca Valley. The winding, four-mile (6.4 kilometer) drive has been designated a California Scenic Drive.

ANTELOPE VALLEY INDIAN MUSEUM

Yato Kya was the name Howard Arden Edwards gave the home he built right into the side of a rock mountain. The most unique part of the home is that there is a natural waterfall in the living room. Edwards designed and constructed the Swiss chalet–style structure into a rock formation known as Piute Butte in the Mojave Desert. When his dream home was completed in

1932, he painted it inside and out with brightly colored American Indian motifs, designs and murals. The floor is the top of an interior rock formation.

Edwards, his wife and son lived in the home until 1939, when he sold it to Grace Wilcox Oliver, a student of anthropology. She also was an avid collector of American Indian artifacts. She remodeled the main building and converted the living quarters into exhibit rooms, including the Katchina Hall. In early 1940, she opened the home as the Antelope Valley Indian Museum, continuing to live there while adding to her collection. She operated the museum for the next three decades. The home today is on the National Register of Historic Places.

In 1979, Oliver sold the museum to the State of California and donated all of its contents. The state parks system then designated the museum as one of its Regional Indian Museums. Its specialty is the representation of cultures of the western Great Basin east and southeast of the Sierra Nevada range.

Today, this unique home and museum is open to the public, where visitors can mosey through the unique structure, peruse the extensive exhibits and hear the melodic flute music in the background. In an adjoining structure known as the Joshua Cottage, there is a touch table and regular demonstrations on fire starting and cooking with native plants. The smell of fresh Indian fry bread may permeate the air, or an educational program might be in session. In the main house, there is a gift shop where visitors may purchase authentic Native American handcrafted jewelry, Kachina dolls, pottery, rugs and a large selection of publications for all ages on Native American history and culture.

The museum is located in Lancaster near Avenue M between 150th and 170th Streets at 15701 East Avenue M.

China Ranch and Date Farm

Visiting this charming ranch is not only a history lesson but also a delicious experience. Located in a historic Mojave Desert area near Tecopa California, it abuts the Old Spanish Trail traveled by explorer John Frémont in the spring of 1893 and the historic Tonopah and Tidewater railroad bed. The public is invited to visit this family-owned working farm and learn about the history of the date business. The address is simply China Ranch Road, Tecopa.

The ranch is an oasis surrounded by a dry sandy desert. The lush trees are evidence of plentiful water. Visitors are invited to hike the trails through the forest areas and sit by clear ponds teeming with fish. Here you may see a fox, a coyote or a rabbit. The area is a popular stopover for migrating birds.

Since the turn of the century, the ranch has changed hands many times, not always in an amicable manner. The property was purchased in 1970 by Charles Brown Jr. and Bernice Sorrells, the son and daughter of area pioneer and longtime state senator Charles Brown of Shoshone, and the ranch remains in that family today.

In the early 1920s, the date grove was planted by Vonola Modine, the youngest daughter of Death Valley–area pioneer R.J. Fairbanks. The flourishing grove can thank the female trees that yield from one hundred to three hundred pounds of dates in season for its success.

On the property is an adobe house that took five years to build. It was built from more than eighteen thousand handmade adobe bricks and completed in 1991.

After perusing the grounds, visitors stop at the store and gift shop where samples of a variety of dates are available as well as date nut bread, muffins and cookies. And of course, a freshly whipped up date shake is a must. This unique farm is a joy to visit.

DARWIN

We call them desert rats, but perhaps they are just ordinary folks who like their privacy and wish to live away from the bustling crowds. If you visit the unique semi-ghost town of Darwin, you will probably not see any of its fifty current inhabitants, but you might notice a parting of curtains and a watchful eye as you walk by.

Once the largest town in Inyo County in the Mojave Desert, it began in about 1860, when a group of prospectors was searching for the rumored Lost Gunsight Mine, which was also tantalizingly called the Mountain of Silver. With success in finding silver-rich outcroppings, the group returned home with stories of its find, and soon prospectors from all over descended on the area filing claims. This was the beginning of the mining town that became Coso Junction. The town of Darwin began to grow and was named after an early explorer named Darwin French.

It didn't take long for the town to become a hub of activity with hundreds of residents. Soon it boasted two smelters and more than twenty working mines. Becoming more sophisticated, Darwin was home to three

Once the largest town in Mojave Desert's Inyo County, Darwin enjoyed great successes until hit with a wave of smallpox deaths and then a widespread fire. It is today a favorite town to explore for history buffs, artists and photographers.

In Darwin today there is much evidence of its mining heyday. Some fifty residents still call it home, but the population swells when visitors stroll through the streets in search of historical scenes.

restaurants, a post office, a newspaper and more than two hundred houses. The population grew to more than 1,000 residents, and later it peaked to 3,500, making it the largest in Inyo County.

Supported by several mines in the area, Darwin counted most on the Defiance Mine. Enjoying profitable years and a growing town, the people were hit with tragedy. A smallpox epidemic coupled with a national economic downturn hit the thriving town hard. As businesses began to close and mines reduced their crews, it looked as though the town of Darwin would die.

There were those who continued to live in Darwin, which by that time must have been a small, close-knit community. For a brief while, there was a resurrection of the good life, and new businesses began to open. However, once again, tragedy struck by way of fire, and again Darwin lost its footing.

Today, there are approximately fifty inhabitants in a town that sees an influx of curious visitors during the mild times of the year. So much of the town's history remains in the form of decaying buildings, mining camps and rusted-out cars and equipment. To some, these items are junk; to others, they are fodder for photographs and reflection. Here you can see what was a glorious past—the hopes and dreams of those who earned their money in the mines and enjoyed a town that was seemingly going to last forever. Here, among the strewn-about artifacts, you might find a piece of a gingham dress, a broken mirror or a tattered schoolbook. It fires up the imagination and delivers the message that nothing lasts forever.

Darwin is but one of the many mining towns that lived and died. It is not a tourist trap or a Disney ride but the remnant of a real town with a colorful history.

This semi-ghost town is located twenty-five miles from Keeler, California.

TRONA'S DIRT

Surrounded by two military sites, a large chemical company and a hardscrabble town, the golf course of Trona is a curious site. When visitors arrive with clubs, they might notice that no one is there to greet them or take their money. After dropping five bucks in the bucket, players walk out to the fairway and suddenly notice something else is missing: grass!

This nine-hole public course is a bit different than most. There is often no staff around so it may be a do-it-yourself day of golfing. Volunteers maintain the course. Golfers are allowed to tee up fairway shots and

The California deserts offer vast views of uncluttered land that melt the stress and anxiety of city life. Brilliant sunsets attract photographers, rugged canyons beckon hikers and lost mines and ghost towns titillate historians.

The heat, desert sky and subtle hues greet desert visitors throughout the year, but it is the spring, when brilliant wildflowers sprout from sandy soil, that pleases visitors most. It is then that prone photographers snap their cameras at belly flowers and bask in acres of fragrant colors.

A brilliantly colored fifty-foot-high mound known as "Salvation Mountain" rises from the desert floor near the Imperial Valley town of Niland, southeast of the Salton Sea. This folk art masterpiece was created by a gentle soul who wanted nothing more than to show his love for God and man.

Salvation Mountain's creator, Leonard Knight, was happy to lead tours and invite visitors to climb his mountain and discover the rooms and coves hidden therein. With never a charge or a sermon, he lived a Spartan life with no amenities and only accepted tips if offered. He began his project in 1985.

An airstream trailer on the Salvation Mountain property may have been used by helpers who assisted Knight during his waning years.

When the World War II marine barracks were abandoned at Camp Dunlap near the town of Niland, a new world began to unfold that is known today as Slab City. It is called "the last free place to live in America." There are no normal amenities in Slab City. It is said to be a close-knit community and is located near Niland.

Giant Rock, a seven-story-high boulder in the Mojave Desert town of Landers, was home to German immigrant Frank Critzer. Living under the rock, Critzer was accused of treason and blown up by FBI agents. The nearby alien landing strip and the giant rock became the scene of UFO conventions. The rock inexplicably broke apart during an earthquake and was painted magenta by vandals to resemble a giant pair of lips.

In honor of travelers in the area throughout time, Bert Vaughn constructed the Desert View Tower. Sections of the "old plank road" that once traversed the nearby area are incorporated into the tower construction. The tower is in San Diego County near the towns of Jacumba and Ocotillo.

Right: Boulder Park located adjacent to the Desert View Tower features stone-carved statues of a variety of creatures created by W.T. Ratliffe. The canyon is designated as California Registered Historical Landmark No. 939.

Below: Cabot Yerxa, known as an explorer, visionary and champion of human rights, is remembered today as hundreds tour the Pueblo Museum he built in Desert Hot Springs.

Left: Above Cabot Yerxa's Lodge sits Waokiye, a forty-three-foot tall carving of a feathered Indian, one of many statues carved by Peter Wolf Toth. An immigrant from Hungary, Toth carved statues for all of the states in the United States, calling his artwork "The Trail of the Whispering Giants." His goal was to pay back the country that took him in and to call awareness to the spirit, culture and plight of the Native Americans.

Below: The little charismatic pupfish resemble a pack of puppies as they swim playfully in their Devils Hole home. They are a distant relative of a type of fish found in this area thousands of years ago when the land was covered with lakes and streams.

Perhaps the most intriguing sculpture in the Gallata Meadows Sky Art of Borrego Springs is the fanciful dragon. The 350-foot serpent's head is framed in flaring horns and tentacles. His body undulates above and below the desert floor, crossing under the road and terminating in the rattle of a snake. Scary on one hand, the monster is beguiling at the same time.

The historic mining "town" of Cerro Gordo sits on a saddle of the Inyo Mountains across Owen's Valley from the Sierra Nevada Range. The American Hotel, said to be the largest hotel in California east of Owen's Valley, was erected in 1871 and stands strong today.

Storefront hours on the main drag of Randsburg are lax. Some are open at "9ish" and close at "5ish." This mining town is visitor friendly with a picnic area and public restrooms. The general store soda fountain is a good place to watch the staff whip up malts in the old-fashioned machines.

Customers traveling to Zzyzx, including Hollywood stars, were greeted by the mineral springs sign, a name they could find at the end of a phone book. Today, the famed sign remains in storage at the site.

Above: The Keys Ranch in Joshua Tree National Park is open for tours that take visitors on a day in the life of those who made the desert their home. The Keys family grew up on the ranch and learned to deal with the hardships.

Right: Bill Keys shot and killed Worth Bagley and went to jail for his crime. He was freed at the behest of lawyer and author Erle Stanley Gardiner. Bagley's headstone reads, "Here is where Worth Bagley bit the dust at the hand of W.F. Keys, May 11, 1943."

Rising 650 feet above the desert floor, the Kelso Dunes are another local example of a "singing dune." Climbing the soft ridged sand is a contemplative experience devoid of motorized dune vehicles.

The Nipton Hotel, located on the northeastern edge of the Mojave Preserve, was built between 1904 and 1910 and restored in 1986 and again in 1994. It offers a glimpse of what hotels and trading posts were like during California's mining days.

Above: Built in the Swiss chalet style, the home of Howard Arden Edwards in Lancaster is now the Antelope Valley Indian Museum. It is built into the side of a rock formation called Piute Butte and features a natural waterfall in the living room.

Right: The Antelope Valley Indian Museum houses the lifelong Native American artifacts collection of Howard Arden Edwards and that of a more recent owner named Grace Wilcox Oliver. The house features a Katchina Hall and a gift shop.

The charming China Ranch and Date Farm sits near the Old Spanish Trail near Tecopa. Visitors can visit the historic buildings, the shaded river trail, the date groves and a gift shop that features date breads and shakes.

On the "Sagebrush Annie" stretch of Route 66 in Helendale, Elmer's Bottle Tree Ranch is a forest of bottle trees, folk art, old signs and other desert art.

The Daggett Garage, also known as Fouts' Garage, is one of the photo stops in the deteriorating town. Built in the 1880s as a locomotive repair roundhouse, it was relocated a few times and is now memorialized in a plaque erected by E Clampus Vitus, Billy Holcomb Chapter No. 1069.

Once a life-giving oasis for the Native Americans located near what is now Joshua Tree National Park, the inhabitants abandoned the precious water source when nearby mining operations chopped down the trees and tapped the spring.

Located in the Coachella Valley Preserve System, the Thousand Palms Oasis is today home to the protected fringe-toed lizard. A visitors' center and miles of trails invite those who wish to remain cool on a hot desert day.

On I-10 west of Palm Springs, motorists are thrilled to spy giant dinosaurs at Cabazon. The original gigantic figures were created by Claude K. Bell, noted sculptor and portrait artist. Today, the four-story museum is a favorite stop for motorists, especially those with child passengers!

Above: While rocks painted to resemble animals are usually cleaned up, this monster rock in the Alabama Hills near Lone Pine has remained for years and is usually the backdrop for photos by passersby.

Right: To commemorate the great camel expedition led by Lieutenant Edward Fitzgerald Beale in 1847, Bert, a celebrated dromedary, trekked the Mojave Road just east of the California-Nevada border near Laughlin.

Left: Unfortunately, Forever Marilyn turned out to not be forever. After a stay of almost two years, the nearly three-story-high statue that graced Palm Springs, the subject of thousands of photographs a day, was hauled off for her next assignment.

Below: Desert dwellers expect many things to surround them, such as extreme climates, howling coyotes, dust storms, flash floods and searing rays of the sun. But most of all, they expect brilliant sunsets decorating the fading light of sky in myriad colors.

are permitted to bring grass mats to save wear and tear on their clubs. Nonmembers are welcome.

It may be the one course at which a golfer needs to look around before proceeding to be sure not to run into a coyote or rattlesnake.

The gateway city to Death Valley, Trona is not only known for its dirt golf course, but likewise, the Trona High School football field is grassless. Called "the pit," the field is home to the Trona Tornadoes. The local players are used to it, but should a team visit, the complaints multiply. The field is watered on game day and then leveled. They say the hard dirt field gives the home team an advantage.

Trona may be the last all-dirt high school football field in the nation.

Another thing you might notice about the town of Trona—it stinks. Well, not a sickly sort of smell, but more of a chemical or sulfur odor. They do, however, have a charming historical museum.

PART III

Remnants of Route 66

Hundreds of examples of desert art, ingenuity and struggles borne by motorists headed west on Route 66 are still to be found in the deserts of California, and most are visible from the road. Relics of roadside attractions still stand, bent under the desert sun. Iconic signs point to enterprises that once were the hopes and dreams of those who serviced Route 66 traffic. There are motels that continue to serve the public today while others have withered and all but disappeared. Rusted cars abandoned roadside tell stories of times gone by.

ELMER'S BOTTLE TREE RANCH

More of a modern roadside attraction, this wayside curiosity is on the Sagebrush Annie stretch of Route 66 in Helendale. It is a photographer's favorite. Wade through the forest of bottle trees and become mesmerized by the wavy light rays piercing through colored glass under the desert sun. Beyond bottles galore, there are folk art, sculptures, industrial equipment, car parts and old signs weaved together in artistic fashion.

This endeavor may satisfy the cravings of those who miss a vanished Route 66 icon called Hulaville. That half-acre outdoor entity belonged to Miles Mahan (1896–1997) and was also known as Mahan's Half Acre. Colorful bottle art, old signs, dolls, a boot hill and a driving range all surrounded Mahan's camp, which consisted of a camper shell. A large wooden sign of a Hawaiian dancing girl marked the spot with a sign below her that read, "People travel through the state, how little will they know her fate, for travelers who'll ever be the wiser, her life was saved by the Supervisors."

When Miles died in 1997, his venture collapsed and was later removed. Remnants are on display at the Victorville Route 66 Museum.

Elmer's Bottle Tree Ranch is located at 24266 National Trails Highway, Oro Grande. There is no entrance charge, but a tip for Elmer is the usual fare.

Polly Gas Sign

An envious recollection of gas prices gone by is evoked by the sight of the Polly Gas sign on old Route 66 near the Helendale store and beer bar. When the interstate was completed, little traffic remained on this road, and consequently, the station closed. For history's sake, the current owner of the station had the sign restored. Polly seems to be bragging while she displays the price at the time: "REG. 18.9 ETHYL 21.9."

On Route 66 between Victorville and Barstow, a Polly Gas sign remains. For history's sake, the owner had it restored.

Auto Club Fountain

Only a few feet off the road on Route 66 in the Mojave Desert town of Essex, a strange sight will greet you. Is it a wishing well? Well, it's something motorists once wished for, that's for sure. This life-saving shingle-roofed structure was installed by the Auto Club of Southern California to be used by motorists along Route 66 for both drinking and filling radiators and the iconic canvas water bags. Cars at that time were subject to all sorts of problems, especially in the desert where daytime temperatures soar above one hundred. For several decades starting in 1926 when the mother road was dedicated, motorists often opted to drive through the desert at night. Day or night, water in Essex was so scarce that free water was not even offered in restaurants. This fountain was a lifesaver.

The fountain remains today as a reminder of the history along the mother road. It is out of order and a bit cockeyed but still intact. It sits just feet off the highway in plain sight as a reminder of the hardships suffered by motorists of the past.

Water in the Mojave Desert town of Essex was in such short supply for motorists along Route 66 during the hot desert days that the Auto Club of Southern California installed a water fountain. Resembling a wishing well, the fountain is a bit cockeyed and no longer works but remains as a reminder of the hardships suffered by motorists in times gone by.

THE STONE HOTEL

This weed-infested, faded relic is located in the town of Daggett, formerly called Calico, a town that was once the major thoroughfare into the town of Barstow. It was named after John Daggett, lieutenant governor of California (1882–86). He was also the owner of the Bismark Mine in Calico. Daggett was originally populated by miners, serving as a supply center.

Today there is not much left in Daggett, sad for a town that was once destined to become a major community before it was eclipsed by Barstow.

Crumbling behind a fence, its explanatory signboard missing, the 1875 Stone Hotel earned its place in history not for what it was but for one patron in particular. It is difficult to think of naturalist John Muir without picturing him in the mountains climbing a pine tree. But Muir was a regular visitor to this Mojave Desert town because his daughter, Helen, lived there. Ordered by her doctors to move to a place where she could live in a warm, dry climate, she made Daggett her home.

In 1914, Muir visited his daughter and spent a few days in Daggett although he was not feeling well. He returned to Los Angeles and died a few days later.

The Stone Hotel of Daggett, a town eclipsed by Barstow, was a regular hangout for naturalist John Muir. His daughter, Helen, lived in Daggett to take in the desert air to heal her respiratory ailments, and Muir came often to visit her.

Besides Muir, it is said that Wyatt Earp strolled the streets of Daggett as well as Death Valley Scotty and Shorty Harris, who frequented the hotel to plan their mining operations. Barney Oldfield also sped through town in a race.

Fouts' Garage

A favorite photo spot in the town of Daggett is the Daggett Garage, also called Fouts' Garage. It reeks of the past and brings history alive. Built in the 1880s as a locomotive repair roundhouse for the narrow-gauge Borate and Daggett Railroad, it was located on Calico Dry Lake but was later moved via a twenty-mule team to the Waterloo Mill and Mine. In 1912, the building was again relocated to the site in Daggett where it stands today.

A plaque erected in 2003 by Billy Holcomb Chapter No. 1069, E Clampus Vitus, and the Daggett Historical Society, Inc. (Marker Number 115) on the site recites:

> *The building was an auto repair shop on the National Old Trails Highway until World War II, when it became a mess hall for United States Army troops guarding the local railroad bridges. The Fouts brothers bought the building in 1946 and operated an automotive garage and machine shop in the building until the mid-1980s. The building is currently owned and operated by the Golden Mining and Trucking Company.*

You will note that Daggett is sometimes spelled Dagett or Dagget, and is even spelled in different ways on freeway signs in the area.

The garage is located at the intersection of Santa Fe Street and Fourth Street, and the post office address listed is 35565 Santa Fe Street, Daggett.

California Agricultural Station

A former State Government Agricultural Station building (1930–53) sits abandoned just east of Daggett. The original station was built in 1923 and rebuilt in 1931 and again in 1953. It is the site where director John Ford filmed the scene where the Joad family was stopped by inspectors in the movie *The Grapes of Wrath*. Were the officials looking for fruit? Although it

A former State Government Agricultural Station building (1930–53) is today used for storage. This is the site where director John Ford filmed the scene where the Joad family was stopped by inspectors in the movie *The Grapes of Wrath*. It is located just east of Daggett.

is said to be an agricultural center, in fact it was used, along with similar stations in other states, as a way to stop and turn around "undesirables" at the border. California at the time was facing high unemployment, and a movement called the "bum blockade" was aimed at keeping anyone from entering the state who could potentially take a job away from a Californian.

The stations were manned by the Los Angeles Police Department because it is said that was the one department that could spare officers to "guard the border."

Although Route 66 was thought of as "the road to freedom" for those fleeing poverty, their dreams of finding work in California often met with disappointment. They were treated poorly, called "Okies" and generally shunned. The practice of stopping them at the border, which sometimes included the threat of arrest, was eventually deemed unlawful, and once again the agriculture stations were used to prevent the transport of diseased fruit.

When the interstate was completed, an inspection station was opened closer to the border in the town of Needles.

The building near Daggett was eventually shut down and is now used for storage. It is worth a stop and a photo, if only for the sake of its appearance in the movies.

PART IV

Historic Cemeteries

There are few things more somber than wandering through a cemetery filled with graves and headstones from days gone by. The stories of those who probably lived in a nearby town are etched in headstones, some simple, some ornate. Faded plastic flowers adorning dirt mounds add to the scene.

BAGDAD

Once a bustling railroad town in the Mojave Desert, Bagdad is now lost to the sand with no evidence of its colorful past. Route 66 motorists drive by, taking no notice. Silence embraces the area, broken only by the sound of an occasional train rumbling through. But if you cross the tracks and look carefully, you will find the Bagdad Cemetery.

Roland, who wishes to remain anonymous, stopped at Bagdad to stretch his legs while headed to Las Vegas on business. He climbed up the berm and across the tracks to look out over the vast desert. Something caught his eye—an anomaly among the sandy earth and bramble bushes. He walked on to get a closer look. What he saw saddened him. There before him was a cemetery in much disarray with three of the seventeen graves partially excavated. Was it vandals? A flash flood? Some of the simple wooden crosses were torn apart, and many of the rocks that outlined the graves were missing.

The once thriving railroad town of Bagdad on Route 66 in the Mojave Desert has all but disappeared. A guardian angel maintains the seemingly forgotten cemetery.

It was sad, he thought, that these deceased persons had been robbed of their dignity in death.

Weeks later, Roland returned to the spot, this time armed with a rake. He replaced the missing rocks, repaired the wire on the wooden crosses and raked the grounds. Thereafter, on his frequent trips to Las Vegas, he made it his responsibility to keep the cemetery in good shape. He hid his rake in some bushes, and once when he returned it was missing. Someone must have also found this spot. Undeterred, he executes his responsibility regularly and has made it his mission in life to keep the cemetery in good shape.

The town of Bagdad was founded in 1883 when the Atchison, Topeka and Santa Fe Railway Line between Barstow and Needles was constructed. The town was eventually abandoned and the structures removed in 1991. It is said that Bagdad boasted the only dance hall in the area. It is also famous for the Bagdad Café. The 1987 German movie entitled *Bagdad Café*, starring Jack Palance and Marianne Sagebrecht, aired and quickly became a cult film. It was not, however, the actual café that was located in Bagdad that appeared as the café in the movie. It was the Sidewinder Café located in Newberry Springs that was renamed the Bagdad Café for the movie. The Sidewinder was permanently changed to the Bagdad Café and is a favorite spot for Route 66 buffs to frequent.

SHOSHONE

This small hillside cemetery just south of Shoshone contains about seventy graves, most well marked with etched gravestones. It can be seen from State Highway 127.

The town of Shoshone was founded in 1910 by Ralph Jacobus Fairbanks, affectionately called "Dad." He was a prospector and bent on building businesses along the Tonopah and Tidewater Railway Line. Eventually, he took off to live in Baker, but his son-in-law, Charles "Charlie" Brown, who became a California state senator in 1927, took over management of the town. The job was later turned over to his son.

The word Shoshone is from *sosoni*, which means land of the tall grass. The Timbisha Shoshone Tribe are the native people of the Death Valley area.

The area is near the junction to Death Valley in the Mojave Desert. Shoshone celebrates the town's uniqueness with an annual event dubbed "Shoshone Days." The Crowbar Saloon, the museum and the general store are stopovers for motorists passing through. The area is known as the Amargosa River Valley.

The cemetery is fenced, but a gate allows access.

The town of Shoshone near the junction to Death Valley in the Amargosa River Valley maintains a small graveyard. Visitors can find their imaginations piqued as they read the headstones and peer through a window into local history.

AMBOY

A small cemetery may be found in the town of Amboy. This Route 66 spot is called the town that wouldn't die. Miles from I-40, it withered when Route 66 was decommissioned and motorists opted for the new and bigger highway. But more and more these days, motorists are taking road trips on Route 66 for the express reason of experiencing a stop in towns like Amboy. Often the gas station is crowded with bikers from Brazil, RVers from Germany, as well as Americans rediscovering the mother road.

In existence since the late 1800s, it served as a railroad depot as well as a welcome stop for travelers who would eat at Roy's Café and stay in the small hotel.

Amboy, the Mojave Desert Route 66 town that refuses to die, is slowly on its way to resurrection. Visitors usually stop at the local graveyard to offer respects and take photos.

PART V
Historic Oases

Oasis of Mara

The Serrano Indians called it "the place of little springs and much grass," and so it is today. A delightful haven and respite from the blazing summer sun, both the Serrano and Chemehuevi populated the springs, having been told by a medicine man that living there would ensure that an abundance of baby boys would come forth. It is said that each time a baby boy entered their world, they would plant a palm tree.

This mystical half-mile-long oasis was formed by the Pinto Mountain Fault line approximately nine thousand years ago. It began to decline in the 1870s when prospectors descended on the area in search of gold. Several mines were worked, including the Desert Queen and the Lost Horse Mines. Needing timber for their operations, the mineworkers began felling the trees and tapping into the water at the oasis. Cattlemen followed and then homesteaders, and eventually, an adobe house was built near the spring. By 1913, the entire Native American population at the oasis had abandoned the area.

Today, the oasis is well cared for on the property of the Twentynine Palms Inn, an establishment dedicated to the art of relaxation. The eastern end of the oasis property is just behind the Joshua Tree National Park visitors' center.

Visiting the oasis today is a delightful experience. Sitting below the shade of the palms, you can see turtles, frogs and an abundance of birdlife, such as green herons, ruddy ducks, roadrunners and owls.

The adobe house still stands near the pond, and hiking trails lead to areas around the grounds, some offering magnificent desert views.

Thousand Palm Oasis

You can smell the cool before you see the pool. The Thousand Palm Oasis is a gem, especially under a blazing desert sun. Located in the Coachella Valley Preserve System, it offers over twenty-five hiking trails, and whether you choose a short jaunt below the palms or a strenuous hike into the canyon, you will appreciate the clear waters babbling through.

This twenty-thousand-acre sanctuary protects the endangered Coachella Valley fringe-toed lizard and sits atop the San Andreas Fault. It is the fault that causes the underground spring waters to flow to the surface, and it is these waters that have attracted thousands of visitors from back in the days the Native Americans roamed freely in the area.

On arrival, it pays to stop by the visitors' center to learn about what the oasis offers and where the trails lead. The cool, dark stone building built from vertical palm trunks was homesteaded by Albert Thornburg in the year 1900 and five years later traded to Paul Wilhelm for two mules and a wagon. The oasis has been open to the public since 1984.

The visitors' center contains vintage photos of the area, exhibits and a staff to answer questions.

A short hike on a boardwalk above the spring waters winds through a shady stand of desert fan palms, *Washingtonia filifera*, the only palm native to the western United States. The palms tower above the waters, their trunks partially covered by long dry skirts that serve as home to desert dwellers. Purportedly, the temperature can be twenty degrees cooler below these palms than in the exposed areas nearby. A specie of the unique desert pupfish darts about freely in the clear waters.

A longer hike will take you to the McCallum Oasis, about a two-mile round trip on sandy terrain.

The oasis is managed by the Nature Conservancy, Bureau of Land Management, Wildlife Service, California Department of Fish and Game and the California Department of Parks and Recreation. Admission is free, and guided hikes are offered throughout the day. There are picnic tables and free parking.

PALM CANYON OASIS

Another oasis that brought life-sustaining conditions to the Agua Caliente Cahuilla Indians is today open to the public though on reservation land. Perched on a ledge is a trading post that sells hiking maps, refreshments and Indian art. The short jaunt down to the spring-water river delivers you to a hiking trail shaded by the California fan palm trees (*Washingtonia filifera*). The actual trail stretches fifteen miles through indigenous flora and fauna, which the Cahuilla treasured as a life-source. Looking carefully, you might find evidence of past life in the canyon such as rock art, grinding pits, irrigation ditches and foundations.

There is a fee to enter the reservation, and operating hours depend on the time of year. This area is deemed to be one of the great beauty spots in Western North America.

Shaded by California fan palms (*Washingtonia filifera*), the Palm Canyon Oasis was inhabited by the Agua Caliente Cahuilla Indians, and though it is on reservation land, visitors are invited to hike along the cool-water shores. It is located near Palm Springs.

PART VI

Desert Art

Coso Petroglyphs

Desert art comes in many forms from ancient to modern. For thousands of years, man has communicated through drawings on rocks, leaving a mark that tells a story. The petroglyphs of the Coso Rock Art District are about as ancient as it gets. There are more than 100,000 Native American petroglyphs in this northern edge of the Mojave Desert. The area includes the Big and Little Petroglyph Canyons, which were declared a National Historic Landmark in 1964 and incorporated into a larger National Historic Landmark District in 2001. That area is known as the Coso Rock Art District.

These petroglyphs decorate the walls of a narrow canyon and are said to be as old as sixteen thousand years and as recent as the 1800s. Although scientists have certainly researched their origin, no one really knows who was responsible or why they chose this particular area. The Coso Range is situated between the Sierra Nevada on the west and the Argus Range to the east. The Owens Dry Lake lies to the north and Wells Valley to the south.

A petroglyph, or engraving on rock, is created by incising, picking or carving on a rock's surface; breaking through the dark patina on a rock, the light color beneath is exposed. This form of art appears worldwide, and the figures have been heavily studied.

The Coso Range petroglyphs, also called rock engravings, seem to depict six major categories of images: bighorn sheep, entoptic images, humanlike figures that are predominately male, a variety of animals, fighting and tools.

There are more than 100,000 Native American petroglyphs on the northern edge of the Mojave Desert. The Coso area is considered sacred and is protected by the China Lakes Naval Weapons Base.

The predominant artwork is of bighorn sheep, which are still prevalent in the area.

The area was most certainly considered sacred and was also used as a place to meet to trade with other peoples. It is said that shamans visited from as far away as Utah to commune with the spirit world in the area. It is fortunate that the naval base serves as a guardian of the ancient rock art, or most certainly the petroglyphs would be ruined by now.

Imagine strolling through the canyon and experiencing a close encounter with thousands of ancient petroglyphs. This is possible but within the parameters of the local protection efforts. The canyons lie on the China Lakes Naval Weapons Base, and visitors are required to register. Access to the lower Renegade Canyon, also called little petroglyph canyon, may be arranged through the Maturango Museum in Ridgecrest. Guided tours are conducted throughout the spring and fall months with a maximum of fifty guests per tour. The address for the museum is: 100 East Las Flores Avenue, Ridgecrest, California, 93555.

Aside from the petroglyph tours, the museum is an attraction in itself and worth an hour's time to peruse. Revolving exhibits on local history and wildlife, an art gallery and a gift shop are featured.

DESERT ART

GRANITE MOUNTAIN PICTOGRAPHS

At the convergence of the Mojave, Sonoran and Great Basin Deserts in what is now eastern San Bernardino County, there is a wide area once inhabited by hunter-gatherers and later the Mohave and Chemehuevi, all drawn to the area because of numerous springs and an abundance of plant and wildlife.

This area of the Granite Mountains contains one of the largest collections of prehistoric rock art in the Mojave Desert and is one of the densest concentrations of painted rock art. Deemed to be sacred land, wonderful examples of pictographs and petroglyphs are widespread.

While petroglyphs are created by etching on rock, pictographs are described as signs or symbols painted on rock. Paint was made by mixing ground-up pigments such as hematite, limonite or charcoal. The mixture also included a binder such as blood, animal fat, egg white, fish or plant oil. Pictographs are often created by using brushes or substituting fingers for a brush.

Because pictographs are more prone to damage due to weather conditions, they are usually found in outcroppings or caves where they are protected. However, it is unknown how many examples of this ancient art style have been desecrated by man.

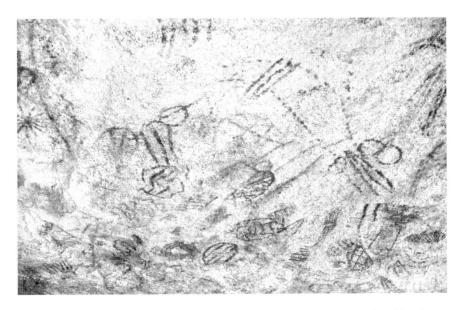

The area of the Granite Mountains contains one of the largest collections of prehistoric rock art in the Mojave Desert. These pictographs are created with paint while petroglyphs are created by etching.

One such example that remains for all to see is the result of damage to an ancient pictograph in the Barker Dam area of Joshua Tree National Park. The Disney Studios were in a small cave filming a movie entitled *Chico, the Misunderstood Coyote*. The ancient pictograph did not show up well for filming so the crew painted over it to make it more visible. This was in the late 1950s and of course would never be repeated by a reputable film crew today. It is, however, an example of the loss of an ancient pictograph. The popular hike to Barker Dam includes a return trail to the parking lot that takes you right to this pictograph cave and the painted-over example.

Cabazon Dinosaurs

To the thrill of children bored on the road, two giant dinosaurs rise skyward at Cabazon on I-10 west of Palm Springs. Subject of movies, commercials and tour books, these monster sculptures are celebrated desert art. They even appeared in the movie *Pee Wee's Big Adventure*. These gigantic figures were created by Claude K. Bell, a noted sculptor and portrait artist. His aim was to attract customers to his Wheel Inn Café. The restaurant opened in 1958, and in 1964 he began to create the first of the dinosaurs, which he named Dinny. It took eleven years to build the forty-foot-high prehistoric reptile out of salvaged materials from a nearby construction site and reportedly cost him $300,000.

Dinny is not just a sculpture to catch the eye of motorists; rather, he is actually a building and today serves as a museum.

Bell created a second dinosaur, the Tyrannosaurus, which added a special feature: a slide down its tail. Unfortunately, Bell died before it was completed. He left a drawing board with many dinosaur statue dreams, never to come true. New owners took over the restaurant, but it closed in 2013.

Today, the roadside attraction is prospering and remains open to the public seven days a week. It features a dinosaur garden and a robotic dinosaur, a four-story museum, an observation tower and, of course, a gift shop. It is said that the dinosaurs attract more than twelve thousand visitors a year.

DESERT ART

TWENTYNINE PALMS MURALS

Many desert towns have taken to featuring historical murals on otherwise blank sides of buildings such as restaurants, stores and even banks. Twentynine Palms, gateway to the Mojave Desert, is one such town and has come to be known as an "Oasis of Murals." The project began in 1994, an epiphany of the local nonprofit public art and beautification committee designed to spark community pride.

This town, located near Joshua Tree National Park, is anchored by the largest marine base in the world: the Marine Corp Air Ground Combat Center. That is probably why there is an abundance of tattoo parlors and barbers throughout town. The murals are lovely and exhibit subtle colors depicting historic memories of the town.

Since early times, people have been attracted to the area for its dry, warm climate. Those suffering from respiratory diseases found the local weather to be therapeutic. Many people, including veterans, brought their families to the area and began homesteading. By the 1930s, the homesteaders, lung patients and miners had built themselves a schoolhouse and general store, and by 1940 the Little Church of the Desert had been constructed. The first edition of the

Twentynine Palms, the gateway town to the Mojave Desert, has earned a reputation as the Oasis of Murals. Historical murals adorn otherwise blank walls, creating visual one-page history books.

Desert Trail newspaper rolled out on April 18, 1935. When the murals began decorating the town, Twentynine Palms became known to the world.

Another claim to fame is the appearance of stars in the town. Actor James Cagney owned a home in Twentynine Palms, and actress Esther Williams was known to visit her brother who resided there.

The first mural created in 1994 was that of Bill and Frances Keys, pioneer homesteaders who settled at the Desert Queen Ranch in what is now Joshua Tree National Park. Bill Keys, a cattleman, gold prospector and assayer, came to the area in 1910. The second mural depicts early life at the Oasis of Mara, a lush palm oasis, showing Cahuilla Indians gathering water among the palms. It also includes surveyors conducting a desert survey.

A number of historic murals have since been created, telling many fascinating aspects of the town's history. A book has been published with photos of the murals and their messages.

BARSTOW MURALS

Murals have begun to pop up around the city of Barstow, a result of its Main Street Mural project. These paintings depict historical events and people of this Mojave Desert town, the crossroads of I-15 and I-40. The

Commemorating Lieutenant Beale's camel experiment is one of the many murals of Barstow's Main Street mural project that began in 1998. The first mural was an image of the Old National Trails Highway and its transition to Route 66.

idea was to create an outdoor walking gallery along "Route 66's Last Existing Main Street."

The first mural appeared in 1998 and depicts an image of the Old National Trails Highway and its transition into Route 66. A jackrabbit, dubbed Rusty Dusty by Barstow schoolchildren, appears in all of the murals, although sometimes it is hidden. Other murals depict Lieutenant Edward Beale and his camel brigade, the Casa del Desierto Railway Station and Harvey House, the Mormon Trail and the Mojave Runners, to name a few.

DANBY MURAL

This Route 66 town was a railroad stop during the era of steam trains. To service passengers and the streams of motorists, a store, café and gas station opened and thrived until the interstate lured fickle drivers away. Although the town has all but disappeared, some foundations and walls remain. On one structure, there is a small mural depicting what appears to be a

The Mojave Desert town of Danby began to melt away when I-40 took traffic away from Route 66. With only a few structures standing, it is fun to see a small mural that remains. It is said that a customer with no money painted the mural in exchange for goods.

mountain man pointing a gun and two additional figures with mountains as a backdrop. It is rumored that a motorist passing through could not afford to purchase supplies and paid for the goods with this artistic talent, resulting in the mural.

PART VII

Transient Roadside Anomalies

Many of the oddities of the desert are established and visited by those searching for adventure. Other curious sites seem to pop up spontaneously, causing motorists to pull to the roadside, take photos and perhaps make a mental note to bring extra shoes the next time they travel that way. They are referred to here as transient because they are in fact a type of graffiti, vandalism or littering. Much of the time if they don't disappear on their own, they are removed by the authorities. Art or vandalism? Whichever, they exist, disappear and often reappear.

SHOE, BRA AND PANTY TREES

A car full of teens pulls off the road, and on a whim, they throw their shoes onto the branches of a nearby tree. After the teens drive off, the footwear dangles in the desert wind, inviting others to join in the fun. Soon the tree is hanging to the ground, burdened by hundreds of tossed shoes and gaining the title "the Shoe Tree." Word spreads.

Just as the tree begins to gain the reputation of a permanent desert oddity, it burns or falls to the ground. Another emerges. And as a tribute to American creativity, a bra tree is established nearby, which in turn grows, attracts and disappears.

While many roadside attractions are permanent, the deserts of California seem to invite fleeting fascinations such as the shoe, bra and panty trees. They pop up and disappear.

ROCK ART

Rock graffiti also seems to become an obsession for travelers. In many areas, especially along Route 66 in the Mojave Desert, the banks of the highway become covered with rock art declaring love framed in rock hearts, names galore and other creative artwork. Although it may be deemed graffiti, it is not permanent and may disappear after the area is inundated with rain.

PAINTED ROCKS

A true form of graffiti commonly spotted alongside desert roads are the lizard or monster rocks painted with eyes, teeth and usually scales. A large-size example is the Giant Rock in Landers. One day, the rock inexplicably fell and broke almost in half. From that time, it resembled a pair of giant lips. To add to the scene, an anonymous person painted the "lips" a brilliant shade of magenta. Deemed graffiti, the magenta was eventually removed.

A large rock that is dubbed the Alabama Hills Nessie can be seen alongside the road out of Lone Pine that ends at Whitney Portals. It is such a popular attraction that the parking area below it is often filled with cars. Adults and children alike hike to the top of the rock to pose for photos.

Are these anomalies true creativity or just a form of littering? The jury is still out on that question.

These oddities come and go. Their fleeting presence is a reminder for travelers to keep out a sharp eye and vigilantly watch the roadside. On desert roads, it is usually easy to pull over to appreciate transient roadside oddities and, of course, snap photos.

Opposite, bottom: Confessions of love, names and simple drawings appear along desert roads, fashioned by rocks, glass and other desert litter. Transient in nature, these creations often disappear as fast as they appear.

PART VIII

Vanished Desert Oddities

Of course, over the years, thousands of desert oddities have disappeared, lost to the elements, vandalized or removed by the authorities. There has always been a rumor about a dried up body in a lawn chair basking in the desert sun, but it is not to be found. And most desert dwellers have heard of the burning tires on a dark road outside of Trona. It seems travelers have spotted this anomaly, run back to town to report the event but then found nothing when they return.

There was the great mushroom-shaped rock in Death Valley that collapsed when a Boy Scout troop climbed to the top for a photo op. The boys survived, but the popular desert oddity was demolished.

For the sake of history, and for entertainment purposes, this chapter sets forth a few personal adventures experienced by the authors. These curious sites are vanished now but were on the unofficial list of the best desert oddities at one time.

Loneliest Telephone Booth

When the back wheels started spinning, I glanced in the side mirror and saw the fine desert sand rising like a mist against the bluest of skies. It was then that it occurred to me that we had broken every desert travel rule. Headed home from a business trip in Las Vegas, it was a spontaneous decision to find a phenomenon that had gained worldwide attention. It was commonly called "the loneliest phone booth in the world."

Bumping down a jeep road in a passenger car, we had no water, no map and no clear direction to our goal, and the gas gauge needle was nearing a rendezvous with the E. But I knew that nagging would do no good. He was on a mission, a quest, an exercise in determination. We had turned off I-15 in a frantic search for this curious booth that we knew was more than eight miles from any numbered highway.

Suddenly, the road seemed to evaporate into a small ranch as we made our way between cows and brambles. I suggested that we stop and ask for directions, but a flash of canine fangs from two agitated hounds quashed that notion, and we bumped along as the road continued. For miles, we saw no cars, no signs and no life save a seemingly dazed bull ambling among the Joshua trees and an occasional crow or meadowlark.

But just as hope was fading, we spied a line of telephone poles, and there before us in all its glory was the notorious phone booth. The glass was missing; it was squattier than most booths and had been adorned with bottles, business cards, a compass, shoestring and loose change. I hopped in to pose for a picture and was startled when the phone rang.

Hello? A thick French accent greeted me. "Is this the phone in the desert?" she asked. "Is this the famous phone in the middle of nowhere?" She explained that she had learned of the Mojave Desert and its celebrated phone from the Internet and news articles. No sooner had I replaced the receiver when another ring reverberated across this sandy stretch of land. The caller was Sandra from Germany, but she spoke no English and we finally gave up on our attempt to converse.

My turn to be the photographer, so my husband jumped into the booth to pose.

Ring, ring.

A lady from Texas was thrilled to get through. She had read so much about this phone. He described to her the deteriorated road we had traversed to reach the booth and was tempted to say we were surrounded by wild Indians but thought better. She offered us a solution. In her research about the booth, she had printed a map so she gave us directions for a safer and quicker road back to the highway. It was ironic that here in the California desert we received directions from a lady in Texas. The road back was not an improvement, however, but fortunately we sailed through the sand without getting stuck.

Finally, we reached the town of Baker, which is known as home to the world's largest thermometer. Stopping for lunch at the Mad Greek, we heard a patron inquire of the waitress: "Hey, do you know how to get to the loneliest phone booth in the desert?"

The story goes that the booth was placed in its desolate spot in 1948 for use by workers at a nearby cinder mine. The rotary dial was replaced in 1970. Inspired by the booth and its reputation, an independent short film titled *Dead Line* was created; a short documentary called *Desert Mirage* and a full-length movie called *Mojave Phone Booth* were made. Long before the booth gained its reputation, the mine was closed. However, in the still of this vast desert, people dialed (760) 733-9969, and as they waited to see if anyone would answer, the ringing sound would float across the desert, heard only by coyotes and phainopeplas.

The phone was removed on May 17, 2000, by Pacific Bell at the request of the National Park Service, and the number was retired. It has apparently now been revived as a conference number where strangers can connect as they did in the heyday of the loneliest phone booth in the desert. Give it a try!

THE CAMEL BRIGADE

Perched on a rock under the desert sky, I scanned the horizon for an approaching lanky camel.

You see, I had a date with Bert, a celebrated dromedary, for a ride along the Old Mojave Road just east of the California-Nevada border.

One of the most colorful historic episodes to occur on the Mojave Road was the great camel expedition led by Lieutenant Edward Fitzgerald Beale in 1857. As the story goes—and the details have been challenged—several breeds of camels were imported from the Middle East to test their effectiveness as pack animals along the desert trails of the West.

Commissioned to survey a wagon road from Fort Defiance, New Mexico, to the Colorado River, Lieutenant Beale took along twenty-five camels and later continued the camel trek to Fort Tejon in California.

Although Lieutenant Beale reported that the camels performed well, their worth was questioned because they tended to scare the horses, which were held in high esteem. Ultimately, the camel experiment was considered a failure.

Jolted by a far-off sound, I suddenly spied movement and then focused on an extraordinary sight—the modern-day camel trek was headed my way. Wisps of fine desert sand floated in the air as two vehicles led a procession to ward off any wayward dirt bikers who might spook the animals.

Lumbering behind was doe-eyed Bert, appearing rather bored but regal, with a red blanket draped over his hump. He was ridden by his owner, Nance Fite, a reserve deputy with the San Dimas, California Sheriff Department Horse Patrol. It is said that Bert himself was once presented with a deputy identification badge and is a member of the city's sheriff's posse, a fact that got him into the *Guinness Book of Records.*

My turn has come. Nance yells, "Koosh," and Bert obediently lowers himself to the ground. His front knees buckle into the sandy path, and he then neatly folds his hind legs. I note a green slimy dribble escaping his mouth, glistening in the desert sun. Warily, I climb on, and as his back legs straighten, I nearly do an "endo" somersault over his head, but I hang on and manage to stay put.

Once on the path surrounded by horses and vehicles, I looked down and realized how high off the ground I was, wondering if I should have worn a helmet. Bert's gait was steady and comfortable as our parade proceeded into the vast open desert. A short time later, it was time to debark, and my adventure ended.

I had joined a reenactment of the camel brigade sponsored by the Friends of the Old Mojave Road, an organization based in the town of Goffs on Old Route 66. We were in Goffs for the annual rendezvous of the Friends, and I was thrilled at the opportunity of a short but exciting camel ride.

Farewell, Marilyn

As the good people of Palm Springs stood crying in the street, their beloved visitor, the Marilyn Monroe statue, affectionately known as "Forever Marilyn," was hauled off. The nearly three-story-high statue had arrived in Palm Springs from Chicago's Michigan Avenue, where it had stood for more than a year.

Thousands upon thousands of photos had been shot of the statue, which appeared in Marilyn's most famous pose with her white dress blowing skyward in the breeze. It was made from painted stainless steel and aluminum yet appeared to be soft and squeezable. She was so tall that even adults posing for a photo next to her high-heeled shoe only reached to about her ankle. She was even lovelier with the brilliant blue desert sky and backdrop of mountains behind her. Weekly free outdoor movies featuring the star were shown at the statue site, and there was always a crowd to watch.

The statue weighed over thirty-four thousand pounds and stood proudly at Palm Canyon Drive and Tahquitz Canyon Way. It was fitting because of the many years Marilyn spent relaxing in this desert community.

The town bid farewell to Marilyn at a Village Fest on March 27, 2014, and off she went to her new home: Grounds for Sculpture in central New Jersey. However, not accepting the divorce without a fight, the Palm Springs Tourist Bureau is negotiating for her return.

Index

A

Amargosa River Valley 107
Amboy 108
Antelope Valley Indian Museum 92
Anza-Borrego 44, 46–50
Arroyo Tapiado 46
Ash Meadows 38, 39, 40

B

Bagdad 105, 106
Bagdad Café 106
Ballarat 88, 89
Barker Dam 116
Barker Ranch 89
Battle of Wingate Pass 82
Bautista de Anza, Juan 44
Bell, Claude K. 116
Bismark Mine 102
Bottle Tree Ranch 99
Breceda, Ricardo 44

C

Cabazon 116
Cabot's Pueblo Museum 33
Cabot Yerxa 33

Cahuilla 111, 118
California Desert National
    Conservation Area 55
California State Park Service 86
California State University Desert
    Studies Center 74
camels 127
Casebier, Dennis 78, 79
Cerro Gordo 67, 68, 70
Chasm Cave 46
Chemehuevi 61, 74, 87, 109, 115
China Ranch 93
Coachella Valley 34, 110
Colorado River 27, 127
Coso 94, 113
Cowboy Man 51, 53
Critzer, Frank 23

D

Daggett 102, 103, 104
Darwin 94, 96
Death Valley Scotty 82
Desert Queen Mine 83, 109
Desert View Tower 32, 33
Devils Hole 37–41
Devils Hole Pupfish 38

INDEX

E

Earp, Wyatt 64, 65, 103
Edwards, Howard Arden 92
Essex 87, 88, 101
Eureka Dunes 58, 59
Eyraud, Cole 34, 35

F

Forever Marilyn 128

G

Giant Rock 23–26, 63, 123
Giant Thermometer 30
Goffs 78, 79, 81, 128
Granite Mountains 115
Great Basin 16, 93, 115

H

Herron, Willis 30
Hollywood 46, 50, 67
Howser, Huell 21, 85

I

intaglios 27
Integratron 23–26, 63
Inyo County 59, 94, 96

J

Jacumba 32, 33
Joshua Tree National Park 81, 83, 109, 116–118

K

Keeler 67–71, 96
Kelso 83–85
Keys, Bill 82, 118
Keys Ranch 81
Knight, Leonard 19

L

Lake Manly 37
Last Chance Canyon 28
Loneliest Telephone Booth 125
Lone Pine 67, 123

M

Manson, Charles 89
Mitchell Caverns 86–88
Mojave Cross 18, 53
Mojave Desert Heritage and Cultural Association 78
Mojave National Preserve 53, 85, 88
Monroe, Marilyn 128
Morongo 63
Muir, John 102
Mystic Maze 35

N

National Mojave Preserve 86
Nature Conservancy 39, 110
Needles 35, 104, 106
Nipton 86

O

Oasis of Mara 109
Ocotillo 32
Old National Trails Highway 119
Oliver, Harry 50
Owens Valley 16, 59, 70

P

Palm Canyon Drive 129
Palm Canyon Oasis 111
Palmer, George 27
Pioneertown 90–92

R

Radcliffe Mine 89
Rand Mine 73
Randsburg 29, 71, 73, 74

INDEX

Red Rock Canyon State Park 30
Ridgecrest 29, 57, 73, 114
Rogers, Roy 90, 91
Route 66 16, 51, 53, 78, 87, 99–108,
    119, 123, 128

S

Salton Sea 21, 44, 51
Salvation Mountain 19, 21, 22
San Bernardino County 16, 22, 23, 78,
    86, 115
San Gabriel Valley 61
Santa Fe Trail 74
Schmidt, Burro 28, 30
Searles Lake 55–57
Serrano 109
Shoshone 94, 107
Sierra Nevada Range 16
Sky Art 44
Slab City 21, 22
Smith, Peg Leg 48–51
Soda Lake 74, 77
Sonoran Desert 16, 26
Southern Pacific Railroad 35
Springer, Curtis Howe 76–78

T

Tahquitz Canyon Way 129
Tapiado Canyon 48
Tehachapi Mountains 16
Thornburg, Albert 110
Thousand Palm Oasis 110
Topock Maze 35, 36
Toth, Peter Wolf 35
Trona 55, 57, 96, 97, 125
Twentynine Palms 61, 81, 82, 109,
    117, 118

U

U.S. Department of Fish and
    Wildlife 39

V

Van Tassel, George 23–25
Vaughn, Bert 32
Vulcan Mine 84

W

Watson, Tex 89
Whistle Stop Café 86
Willie Boy 61–63

Y

Yucca Valley 90, 92
Yuma 32

Z

Zzyzx 74–78

About the Authors

ALAN HELLER has always been under the spell of a hopeless case of wanderlust that began when he was a young boy riding the streetcar into Hollywood alone at the age of ten. He spent his childhood exploring the nooks and crannies of Griffith Park in Los Angeles near the home in

Claudia and Alan Heller.

which he was raised. He led his friends on endless adventures, such as exploring the sewers at the L.A. River areas at night with flashlights fashioned out of tennis ball containers. The Griffith Park Planetarium was a regular haunt. His boundaries widened when he was old enough to drive.

Alan earned a BA in biology at California State University–Los Angeles. He is the immediate past president of Duarte's Public Access Channel (DCTV) and a former commissioner of the Duarte Parks and Recreation Commission, the Duarte Planning Commission and the Duarte Community Service Commission. Alan is a member of the Los Angeles Westerners Corral of History Writers and the Ancient and Honorable Order of E Clampus Vitus, a "disorganization" that places history plaques throughout the West. He is coauthor of *Life on Route 66: Personal Accounts along the Mother Road to California*, having provided the book's photos. Alan's photographs have been published in *Westways Magazine*, *Skin Diver Magazine*, *Route 66 Magazine* and various publications and newspapers.

CLAUDIA HELLER, a bit more sheltered, soon found that dating Alan when they were fifteen years old included adventures she had never considered. With strict parents, she had to be home by 10:00 p.m. When Alan proposed a trip to Mitchell Caverns in the Mojave Desert, she was worried about the time limits. But taking off from Hollywood in the early morning hours, Alan and Claudia took Alan's father's '55 Chevy on Route 66 to the town of Essex in the Mojave Desert and then the circa-twenty-mile road to the caverns. It was an exciting world in the limestone caves, one neither of them had dreamed of. They made it home by curfew.

The eldest of seven children, Claudia grew up in Hollywood, California, and graduated from Los Angeles City College with a degree in journalism. Living in Duarte for the past thirty years, she has served as president of the Duarte Historical Society and Museum for the past twenty years. She writes a bimonthly column for the San Gabriel Valley Newspaper Group in a section of the *Pasadena Star News*. Her columns cover people, events and history of the Duarte area. She is the author of *Life on Route 66: Personal Accounts along the Mother Road to California* as well as *Duarte Chronicles*. She is retired from her career in the legal field and is enjoying retirement.

ABOUT THE AUTHORS

A Lifetime of Adventures

After Alan and Claudia's marriage in 1964, the whole world opened up. There were constraints such as jobs and college and, later, children, but the couple managed to pursue adventures, near and far, at every opportunity. With a tattered army surplus tent and a 1965 Ford, they explored the coast, the desert, the mountains and even places of interest near home, such as downtown Los Angeles. When the family grew, they bought a 1970 El Camino and a camper to top it off and spent the next several years exploring any place they could get to on weekends and vacations. The wanderlust grew, and taking time off life, they drove around the United States for two months, experiencing one adventure after the other.

Finally, the kids were grown and on their own. Alan and Claudia quit their professional jobs on their sixty-sixth birthdays in 2010, bought a small trailer and took off on Route 66 from Santa Monica to Chicago, a trip ripe with new escapades. After penning a series on Route 66 for the *Weekly Star*, a section of the *Pasadena Star News*, the couple published their first book, entitled *Life on Route 66: Personal Accounts along the Mother Road to California*.

In 2013, the couple wrote a second book about the community in which they were living—Duarte, California—entitled *Duarte Chronicles*.

In the year of their fifty-first wedding anniversary, they pulled together descriptions of some of their exciting adventures in their home state of California and fashioned it as this discovery book for those who also suffer from wanderlust. It is designed to help those with the desire to find and explore the sometimes odd, curious and historical sites in the California deserts. Armed with photos and personal experiences gained from all the places in this book, the authors have attempted to bring forth descriptions of the adventures that await those who dare.